SELL YOUR
Crafts
ONLINE

The Handmaker's Guide to Selling on
Etsy, Amazon, Facebook, Instagram,
Pinterest, eBay, Shopify, and More

James Dillehay

ISBN: 978-1-7320264-4-5

Published by:
Warm Snow Publishers
P.O. Box 170
Torreon, NM 87061

Contents

Introduction

Want more online buyers for your handmade products? This book gives you marketing ideas for each of the major platforms so you can decide which is right for you now.

It also shows you how to scale up your sales by selling on multiple platforms when you are ready. As a seller of handmade items, you aren't limited to Etsy, Amazon Handmade, or having your own website, though each of these could provide a substantial business by themselves.

If you can manage a larger business, you can simultaneously run shops on Facebook, Instagram, Pinterest, and other social platforms where shoppers can see your product posts and order directly without leaving the site they are on.

Having multiple stores can feel overwhelming. Here you will discover tools and apps that help you grow and manage your presence on many sites through a single interface.

There are many ideas outlined in these pages. But they aren't here to encourage you to jump on all of them right away. In fact, unless you have already mastered an online marketplace like selling on Etsy first, then aiming for more markets is asking for overwhelm, confusion, and stress.

Read the book through in the order it's written. Make notes of which markets and tools appeal to you. Modify Chapter 5's suggested marketing plan to fit your situation and needs.

Taking random marketing actions here and there will eventually bring in occasional income. But working from a plan brings measurable and sustainable profits in the shortest time. If you want a business that generates money predictably over time, organize your actions around a master plan.

Your plan is your guide, but it's not set in stone, especially with e-commerce, which transforms rapidly. To grow a successful business, adopt an adaptive mindset. Regularly review your progress and edit your plan according to the results of actions you have taken and current circumstances.

Online markets come and go, or change their operating rules. It was a different world when I started selling online back in 1998. Before Etsy, handmakers sold on their own websites or on eBay, AltaVista was a major search engine, and Netscape was the most popular browser. Remember any of those?

In 2000, I wrote a book called *The Basic Guide to Selling Crafts on the Internet*, as part of a *Craft Business Books* series. While a few of the guidelines in that early book have held steady over time, most have changed. I adapted the changes in my own business and now make a good portion of my living from Internet marketing. You can, too.

The University of Alaska hired me to develop an online marketing course they made available to artisans in Alaska. I've taught classes through The Learning Annex, the Bootcamp Marketing for Artists and Craftspeople, and many other places. The lessons I've outlined in this new guide can speed your progress and increase your results.

Many sellers mistake marketing to mean advertising. Paid advertising is only one form of marketing. As my mentor and co-author in a book in the international best-selling Guerrilla Marketing series said, "Marketing is every communication you make about your product or your business."

This new book gives you more ways to communicate, so your products get viewed, remembered, purchased, and recommended.

Before we jump into ways to market your products online, let's get your handmade products business set up.

Chapter 1

Setting Up Your Business

B efore you can make sales online, you need some things in place. This chapter explains basic steps for setting up your business to avoid future problems with the government and to make your online gig operate more smoothly.

Here you will learn about:
- Choosing a name for your business
- Business checking account, business license, and permits
- Accepting credit card payments
- Keeping records

Choosing a Name for Your Business

Your online business needs a short, catchy, memorable name that doesn't already belong to someone else.

Use your business name when creating a website, setting up social media accounts, and legal stuff like a business license and business checking account.

Many makers use their own name as their business name. It's more personal; shoppers can see you are an actual person standing behind your name.

Whether you use your name, or something else, a Google search is the place to learn if anyone is already using the name you want.

If Google doesn't show a business with your choice, next check for registered trademarks at https://www.uspto.gov/trademarks/process/search/ in the US.

In the UK, search trademarks: https://www.gov.uk/search-for-trademark

In Europe, search trademarks: https://www.ipoi.gov.ie/en/ip-search-tools/trademark-search/trade-mark-international-searching/

If you don't find your prospective name registered as a trademark, then do a business name search in your state. Do this by searching the phrase "business name availability (your state's name)."

Usually, this search will bring up your state's business filings bureau where you can learn if anyone else is already using the name you have in mind.

After you have done the research and confirmed that no one else is already using your ideal business name, register it with a business license.

If you don't take steps to ensure your name is not already in use, it could cost you time and money later on should an established business with the same name show up and tell you to cease and desist.

Business Checking Account, Business License or Permit

Since Etsy and many other online marketplaces don't require a business license when you set up a shop, you may wonder why you need to register your business at all.

Income you generate from online sales can be tracked by the government. To avoid problems explaining to them where the money came from, set up your business legally early on when sales come in. Document your income and expenses as evidence you are a legitimate business.

Create a separate business checking account to track your business income and expenses. Most banks require a business license to set up a business checking account.

Also, consider getting a separate credit card to use only for business purchases.

Local business license. Apply at your local county business registration office.

Starting a Business outside the US

For starting and registering a business in Canada, see canada. ca/en/services/business/start.html.

For the UK, visit www.gov.uk.

For Australia, start at register.business.gov.au. Also see business.gov.au/registrations/register-for-taxes/tax-registration-for-your-business

Within the European Union, see europa.eu/youreurope/business/running-business/start-ups/starting-business/index_en.htm

For other countries, Google the phrase "how to legally start a business in (insert your country name)."

Accepting Credit Card Payments

If you plan to sell on Etsy, Amazon Handmade, or other online market, you won't need a credit card processor, because these sites handle transactions and charge you the processing fee. (Those fees are tax deductible expenses.)

If you have your own website, you will need a credit card processor or payment gateway to handle transactions from online sales.

If you sell at craft shows, outdoor markets and festivals, you will need a mobile credit card processor app like those described below.

Does accepting credit cards make a difference? For impulse buys like those at craft shows, the answer is a definite yes. My sales more than doubled when I began accepting cards. A survey showed 83% of businesses report it increased their sales.

Offline sales. Almost 80% of shoppers prefer using a credit card. Mobile apps have made it easy to accept credit cards from just about anywhere.

Using a small card reader that plugs into your smartphone and an app from your card processor, you can key in an item, swipe or insert the card, and have the buyer sign with their finger or a stylus pen.

Two popular mobile credit card service providers are Square at squareup.com and PayPal at paypal.com/us/webapps/mpp/credit card-reader. Both services allow you to accept credit card payments through your smartphone with no monthly charges and only a per-transaction fee. Money from a sale minus the fee is deposited directly into your checking account.

Keeping Records / Accounting

Keep records of your sales along with your expenses. The IRS requires businesses to keep records and file income tax, even when you don't show a profit.

There are different ways of keeping records. If you have a smartphone, there are apps like Expensify that allow you to snap photos of your receipts. If you prefer to make entries by hand, log books for tracking expenses can be found at office supply stores and bookstores.

TaxJar integrates with Etsy shops making it easy to record sales data. Other accounting tools include: Wave, QuickBooks Self-Employed, GoDaddy Bookkeeping for Etsy Sellers, and Zoho.

Examples of expenses you may be allowed to deduct from your business income include: business-related insurance, show rental fees, bank charges, trade periodicals, advertising, office supplies, utilities, contract labor, salaries, equipment rentals or repairs, depreciation, and the cost of goods sold.

Once you have an accounting system in place, it's an excellent practice to back up your files regularly and store them safely. After a computer failed and wiped all my data, I now keep two sets of external hard-drive backups and one online backup account.

Legal and accounting stuff may seem tedious, but doing it right means you can relax and move forward without the worry of future troubles with the government.

When you are setting up or doing a makeover of your business, consider how you will brand it. The next chapter shows how to create memorable branding cues for growing a handmade product line.

Chapter 2

Setting Up Your Online Brand

When preparing to market online, branding can help your items stand out, increase engagement, and boost sales. When promoting online, your presentation has to sell for you. This chapter teaches you how to do that.

Promotional material gives you a way to pass along branding cues so customers remember and refer others to you. Branding includes your story and how you message it. It also includes the use of consistent style elements like fonts, colors, and icons that go into your web pages, social media profiles, and more.

Branding Cues

First impressions are often lasting ones, including business names and logos. Here are the parts that go into building your brand's message. Some of these are mentioned again elsewhere in this guide.

Your Story. People relate to stories. Your story has the potential to pull heartstrings. Mass-manufactured things rarely connect us to actual people behind the products. The buy-handmade and sustainable-fashion trends reveal that shoppers are rejecting factory-made products in favor of individual creativity.

Your Business Name. After you've settled on the name you intend to use, place it throughout your promotional material. Give thought to the name you choose as it will be time-consuming and probably costly to change it later.

Your Authenticity. Large businesses have a problem conveying authenticity. Corporations don't have souls. As a small business, if you are authentic, that's your brand. No one else is like you. All of your choices around logos, fonts, colors, and images can reflect your personality.

Images. Images tell stories. They deliver visuals when you are marketing online and for your display when you are at art or craft shows. You need: product-only images with a white background for online store listings, how-it's-made images, how-it's-used images if needed, lifestyle images showing people enjoying your item, jury images when applying to arts and crafts fairs, and pictures of you to accompany your artist's story. See Chapter 3 for more on photos.

Your Logo. A logo is a small visual that expresses a feeling you want to convey to shoppers. Later in this chapter, you will find where you can design your logo or hire it out to professional graphic designers.

Your Elevator Pitch. In a few short sentences (30 seconds or less to say) what does your product promise customers? For example, a handbag maker promises buyers a "fashion accessory that's practical and stylish."

Fonts and Colors. Consistency is part of good branding. Choose fonts and colors and use those same ones on all your printed materials and website content.

Your Contact Information. Every message you send or promote through should contain information on how people can easily reach you, including your website, phone number, e-mail, and address.

When thinking about how to design your business's look and feel, get inspired by checking out how successful sellers brand their business.

Visit EtsyRank.com where you can browse the top-selling Etsy shops. Under "Competition," choose the category closest to your product line. Check out the successful sellers in your category. How do they use fonts, colors, and logos?

Also, check out sellers on Amazon Handmade bestsellers by category. Choose "Handmade" for your main category and then explore the subcategories closest to your niche and Amazon will show you the top sellers in those areas.

Types of Promotional Materials

Once you have your branding cues created and available, repurpose them again and again in your various promotional materials, like:

Videos. Tell your artist's story with video. Video rules over online marketing. Over 70% (and rising) of shoppers say video influenced their purchases. More than 90% of watchers are likely to remember a call to action on a video. Etsy, Amazon, and most social sites support and encourage product videos to increase sales.

Business cards are among the entrepreneur's cheapest yet most useful tools. Imagine you are wearing something you made when someone crosses paths with you and says, "That is so cute, where did you get it?" You are ready with a business card with all your contact information.

Hangtags. Every piece you sell should have a hanging tag that gives details about your product: the way you made it, simple instructions for product care when appropriate, and something like the words "handmade by" your name.

Thank You cards. With every sale, including a signed Thank You card is a warm, personal touch that customers will appreciate because so many sellers neglect to do it. Include your logo and contact info on the back. When I pack an online order to send out, I place a Thank You card with a coupon for a discount off the customer's next order.

Packaging. Packaging is another opportunity for branding and messaging. Use (and let customers know that you use): biodegradable packaging, upcycled corrugated cardboard, recycled paper, or other biodegradable organic materials.

Postcards make low-cost reminders to mail to previous customers. Cards can include an eye-catching image on one side and marketing message, name, address, and website on the other side. Postcards can help sell new products and close-outs. Mail cards periodically to your customer list. Send out invitational notecards to your mailing list whenever you will be back in their area to do a show or home party. One side of the card has your latest catchy image. Since there's no envelope to decide about opening, customers have to see your photo.

Your voice mail message. If you don't always answer your phone, your voice mail message can communicate a marketing message. Include your website address and perhaps information about an upcoming craft show where you will be displaying. It means updating your message regularly if you do a lot of shows, but it creates the impression of someone who is busy selling.

Checks, return address labels, sales receipts, gift certificates, order forms, and sticker labels provide more opportunities to add a logo, website and promo blurb about what you do. When I accept credit cards at art and craft shows, the customer receives an e-mail or text receipt that includes my business name, a photo of me, and contact information so they can easily remember who they made the purchase from.

Graphic Design Providers

Memorable design in your marketing materials is as important as eye-catching product images. If you want to design your own, the following sites can help with easy-to-use templates:

- Canva.com
- GetStencil.com
- Snappa.com
- Fotor.com
- DesignBold.com

Not sure how to create interesting packaging? Find examples at:

- Flickr.com/search/?q=packaging
- Pinterest.com (search for "packaging design creative.")

If you want to outsource the design aspect, hire designers to do it for you at:

- CreativeMarket.com
- MockupEditor.com
- DesignHill.com
- CrowdSpring.com
- Fiverr.com
- HatchWise.com (logos)
- Etsy.com Search for "logo design" or "banner design" or "etsy shop makeover"

Printing Services

Once you have your designs created, use the following services for fast printing.
- VistaPrint.com
- GotPrint.com
- Moo.com
- Printique.com

Preparing for prime time includes putting attention on your images, one of the most important criteria online buyers cite for why they make a purchase. The next chapter describes how to create photos that do the job of selling for you.

Chapter 3

Images That Sell

Exceptional photos convert more online shoppers into buyers. If you are just starting to gather images or you want to uplevel from what you have been using, look to the images used on successful Etsy shops (EtsyRank.com) and note how their pics are sharp and clear, well-lit, and show off the product from a variety of angles.

There are many, many free tutorials online for improving your product photos and your skills with image software like Photoshop. This chapter links you to the best tips for DIY photography or outsourcing it.

Let's start be defining the six types of product images that help sell your products:

1. **Product-only images with white background** for online store listings. Studies show the white background improves online sales. White background images are required when selling on Amazon, but not on Etsy.

2. **How-it's-made images**. Pictures of you making your products. Shoppers like to see artisans at work. Tell your "how I made this" story through photos.

3. **Step-by-step instructional images** where a person in the photo shows how to use a product, if applicable. My sales doubled when I started including a "how to wear" card with every purchase. The card showed nine different ways to wear the item.

4. **Lifestyle images** showing people in real-life poses enjoying your item. If you can get them, use images of real customers (who have given permission) using your products. You can also use models (found several on Fiverr as mentioned below)

using your item.

5. **Jury images** to submit when applying to arts and crafts fairs. While I'm writing this, many craft shows have canceled due to Covid, but hopefully shows and events will return as a marketing venue.

6. **Head shots** of you to accompany your artist's story in your promotional materials and your social media profiles.

How many photos will you need? The more the better. You can use them for social media posting, product listings, and blog posts. Both Etsy and Amazon let you upload ten images for each product listing. Aim for using all they allow.

DIY Photography Tips

The images you use in your listings may be the single most important influence on converting visitors to buyers. The following tactics will help your images sell for you:

• When selling 3-dimensional objects, include photos taken from different viewpoints so viewers get a sense of depth. Each view should be looking straight at the object. Angle shots make an item look skewed or damaged.

• Take photos in daylight or under Halogen lights (whiter light) or color-balanced lighting.

• Your image colors should be bright with good contrast between dark and lighter areas.

• Digital images can be cropped, color-balanced, contrasted, and enhanced in many ways using a photo-management app.

• For previewing your images, set your own monitor at the highest color resolution. But be aware most computer monitors will view colors slightly different. Older monitors show less accurate color resolution.

• Copying other people's images from Web sites, auctions or print publications is illegal. Unless you see a notice or have evidence that an image is in the Public Domain, assume that every image you see is copyright protected, because the copyright law says an image owner does not have to display a copyright notice; the copyright is legal when the originator creates the image.

If you are on a tight budget or you just want to do your own photography, the following sites offer tutorials:
- join.shawacademy.com/online-photography-course
- alison.com/tag/photography
- youtube.com/user/tutvid/playlists
- bit.ly/PHLearnVids (Photoshop tutorials)

Finding photographers

Commercial product photographers can cost hundreds of dollars. When you engage a professional, you quickly learn they charge additional fees for copyrights as well as the photos themselves. Though you get great pics, you may not have the funds to invest so much money starting out. Cheaper alternatives:

At Fiverr.com I searched for "product photography" and found affordable rates. Copyright is included in the fees. Look for providers with positive reviews and many completed gigs. I only work with those who have received multiple five-star ratings.

Another source for finding photographers is Etsy.com. Type in the search bar: "product photography" for thousands of results. Most services are for product images only, not models. If your product needs a model, expect to pay more.

Also search for "mockup" on Etsy for thousands of examples of products in lifestyle settings.

CreativeMarket.com and DesignCuts.com offer a huge collection of mockups for simulating your product image in a lifestyle setting.

For more craft photography tips, see the resources at: handmadeology.com/big-list-of-product-photography-tips/ and the book, *Photographing Arts, Crafts & Collectibles* by Steve Meltzer.

You've set up your business, begun branding it, and created eye-popping images. How much will you charge for your pieces? An even more important question answered in the next chapter is "how much will buyers pay?"

Chapter 4

Pricing Handmade Items for Online Sales

This chapter teaches you how to price your handmade products for online sales, so you make a healthy profit. Knowing your profit margins guides your choices in where and what you will sell and how you grow your business.

What you will learn:

- Understanding retail and wholesale pricing
- Discovering how much shoppers will pay
- How much it costs you to make an item
- The pricing formula
- Your profit margin
- Pricing one-of-a-kind work

Understanding Retail and Wholesale Pricing

You may sell your handmade pieces in several markets like on Etsy or Amazon, in gift shops, to interior designers, at craft shows and expos, through galleries, or even mail-order catalogs. These markets fall into one of two categories: retail or wholesale. This section describes the different approaches for pricing in each category.

Retail pricing is the amount you ask for a piece when you are selling direct to a customer. Examples of places you might sell retail include art and craft shows, festivals, online through a website, home parties, or from your own studio.

Wholesale pricing is the amount you charge for items you sell to someone else who resells your products to their customers.

For instance, stores, galleries, interior designers, and mail-order catalogs like Sundance Catalog are wholesale markets. Stores price items two to two-and-a-half times what they pay for them.

If you plan to grow your business by selling to stores, knowing your costs and your prices tells you if you can afford to sell wholesale. Imagine having fifty or more stores around the country showing your items five to seven days a week.

There's no definitive answer to whether wholesale or retail is a better business model. I know makers who will not do craft shows, choosing instead to work from home. I know others who only do shows or sell online and never wholesale. And there are other sellers like me who do both.

How Much Will Shoppers Pay?

The question almost every new maker asks is, "How much should I charge for my work?" An even more important question is, "How much will shoppers pay?"

You don't want to lose money by asking only enough to get back your costs when customers will gladly pay higher prices.

To find the average price buyers will pay for pieces like yours, there are ways to survey what is selling where and for how much. This can be an adventure of sorts, going online to browse Etsy or Handmade on Amazon or visiting craft fairs and stores to scope out the marketplace.

You may find the average market price for an item is higher at one place than it is for similar work in a different market(s). For example, a set of wood letters may sell on Etsy at one price, at craft fairs at a different price, and in stores for a higher price.

Below are the major e-commerce sites where you can survey prices for handmade items with a sales history. We only want to look at items with a sales history, because it provides evidence that the item's price was in line with buyer expectations.

www.etsyrank.com. EtsyRank is a subscription service that lets you quickly assess competition of your keywords and products. Type in words closely describing your item and EtsyRank will return related keywords and the top sellers and their prices.

www.marmalead.com. Marmalead, like Etsyrank, is a subscription service providing similar analytics of Etsy keywords, sales, and prices.

www.amazon.com/Best-Sellers-Handmade/zgbs/handmade/ Gives you a listing of the best sellers in the Amazon Handmade category. If the items shown are selling well, their prices are right in line with buyers' expectations.

www.ebay.com. On the left side of the page, under "categories", select "crafts", then look for and click on "handcrafted & finished pieces." Then look for "preferences" and choose "completed listings." On the right side of the results page are completed auction listings of products. Sort the listings by choosing "price: highest first." Look for: (1) products that are selling, (2) number of bids—this shows whether people are eager to buy these crafts, (3) price—shows the highest bid or how much people will pay.

www.sundancecatalog.com. Sundance Catalog is among the most popular mail-order catalogs featuring handmade items. They mail copies to millions of shoppers. Unfortunately, for the craft artist, catalogs want items priced that they can mark up at least four times.

www.artfulhome.com. If you want to sell to interior designers, this is an impressive site to check prices on. Some pieces listed here sell for thousands of dollars.

www.faire.com. A major site allowing handmakers a way to offer their product lines to wholesale buyers. To help store buyers, Faire also shows what items are bestsellers, or in their words, products "flying off the shelf."

www.qvc.com. In the search box, type in a craft item similar to what you make like "birdhouse," "cutting board," "ornament," "decor idea," or just type in "handmade". Note the prices the items sell for. QVC buys in quantity and then resells stuff at a marked up price. QVC has been around on TV since 1986 and has developed the skill of buying items that sell.

Knowing what shoppers are used to paying for craft items like yours, you next need to know your costs for making them.

Cost of Goods or Production Cost

Cost of goods is what you spend to produce the products you sell. Cost of goods includes all material, labor, and overhead costs.

Let's use wind chimes as an example, because they are a steady seller at craft shows and online. "Wind chimes" was searched for over 28,800 times in a recent month on Etsy.

Materials Cost

Your materials include wood, glue, hinges, accessories, and all other supplies needed to complete a project. As an example, say you make wind chimes from wood and recycled materials. For our example, let's say your total materials cost for one set of chimes is $9:

Labor Cost

Cost of labor is the dollar value of the time needed to gather, prepare and produce an item. The cost of labor will be the hourly wage you pay yourself or the wages you pay others as employees or independent contractors.

How much is your time worth? This is something you have to decide, but I wouldn't start lower than $20 per hour.

If you can sell items at a price that would pay you $30, $35, or more per hour, you can profitably hire others at a lower rate (like $15 per hour) to help produce your pieces when sales justify outsourcing labor.

Continuing with the example of the wind chimes, let's say you decided that you value your labor at $20 per hour.

Time needed to arrange materials before assembly: 2 minutes
Time to assemble one set of chimes: 13 minutes
Total cost of labor: .25 hours (15 minutes) x $20 per hour = $5

Note: when you make a piece for the first time, your labor time will be longer. After making several, you will have learned ways to cut the production time. With practice, you'll arrive at the true cost of your labor.

Cost of materials for the wind chimes is $9 and cost of labor is $5, bringing your costs to $14. We now need to account for another, often overlooked cost of doing business commonly known as overhead.

Overhead Cost

Overhead refers to expenses you pay to operate your business day-to-day, even if you work from home. Overhead is also referred to as fixed costs because these expenses remain in a predictable range throughout the year, regardless of how much you sell.

Examples of overhead include: business licenses, rent, utilities, phone, insurance, advertising, office supplies, cleaning supplies, professional dues, and so on.

Calculating all those costs would take time. More established businesses will do the due diligence, but an easy shortcut for a home business is to figure 25 percent of the total of your materials and labor costs to arrive at a number that approximates your overhead.

Adding estimated overhead costs for wind chimes:
$5 labor + $9 materials = $14
$14 x 25% estimated overhead = $3.50

Total production cost for wind chimes:
$14 + $3.5 = $17.50

The Pricing Formula

As you can see in the example above, the total of labor, materials and overhead for making one wind chimes is $17.50.

This is the amount we have to recover to break even. But $17.50 isn't necessarily what you would price your wind chimes at.

Go back to the research you did earlier to learn the average market price for wind chimes. You may find those like yours sell on Etsy or Amazon or at crafts fairs for an average price of $20 or more. Since that's a price that shoppers are used to seeing, you would be in line to price yours at least $20. If you use recycled materials, you can ask a little more, even though your costs are lower. Multiple surveys report that shoppers will pay more to own sustainably produced items (source: Fortune.com.)

Calculating Wholesale Prices

Let's say wind chimes like yours sell in stores for $38. That means they paid $19 or less to the seller. Shops mark up items two to two and half times to arrive at their retail price.

Your break-even cost is $17.50. As long as your wholesale price to stores doesn't drop below $17.50, you can make money selling wholesale.

But what if your break-even cost had been higher, like $20. In a case like that, one needs to:

- Lower material or labor costs, and / or
- Enhance the perceived value of the wind chimes so the store owner will bump up the retail, or
- Switch to making other items that are profitable to sell wholesale.

What's Your Profit Margin?

One of the most important things to learn early on in your business is your profit margin. This amount is the difference between your cost of goods and your asking price.

If your cost of goods is $17.50 and your retail price is $35, your gross profit is $17.50. If you are selling online, that $17.50 gets eaten into by seller fees. You might end up with more like $13 or $14.

Knowing profit margins enables you to make choices for growth by telling you:

- If you can afford to hire help with production, which will allow you to produce more inventory.
- How much money you can spend on ads.
- If you can profitably sell wholesale to stores where you can scale up your business by adding more and more accounts.
- If you can afford to offer free shipping, which will increase your sales.

With all the preparations you have done so far, you are ready to map out where, when, and how you will get your handmade items in front of buyers. The next chapter shows you how to plan and schedule your marketing action steps.

Chapter 5

How to Plan Your Marketing

Everyone has their own vision of how big they want their craft business to become. If you just want a few more sales every month, randomly select tactics from this book and apply them whenever you feel like it.

However, if you are choosing to build a business that sets you financially free from the need for a job, you need a more organized approach. This chapter outlines a proven method for mapping out sustainable, predictable growth.

Your marketing efforts will be more profitable when you understand and define who your most likely customers are, because that will help you learn where those prospective buyers can be found.

For instance, if you make handmade products for children, you want to reach moms, parents, and grandparents. There are plenty of blogs that discuss parenting issues.

If you make organic or recycled crafts, look for eco-minded folks on environmental blogs and sites. An Etsy representative said in an interview in MarthaStewart.com that searches for earth-friendly items was up 43% in all categories.

Suggested Marketing Path for Beginners

If you are just starting to sell online, you have enough things to learn without attempting to take on a multiple marketing venues. Whether you have tried Etsy in the past or just thinking about it, the platform offers many advantages you will discover in Chapter 7.

Think of Etsy as your training ground. Everything you need to learn about online marketing of handmade products you will find from setting up and growing an Etsy shop.

An alternative would be to start with Pinterest, Facebook, or Instagram. Each allows you to create a shop and sell from your posts.

Suggested Marketing Path for Expanding Sales

Scale up your sales by selling on several markets simultaneously. But only look to expand after you have successfully generated regular sales on a single market first. Otherwise, you are likely to feel overwhelmed.

After making sales online on one or two marketplaces, you will have accumulated the skills that will allow you to take on more sites. You'll know the time, because it's when you stop having to figure out how to do every little thing, and your time is filling with making inventory and filling orders. Then is the time to apply the tactics explained in Chapter 16 about selling via multichannel apps.

101 Sample Marketing Ideas

Before you can schedule your marketing communications, you need a list of actions to take. Start with the possibilities in the next section, extracted from the many options in this book. All of these actions may not be appropriate for your specific products, but circle those that are, so you can add them to your calendar or daily planner. You will come up with your own ideas as your business grows. Add your own tactics to the list and to your calendar.

The following suggested actions, grouped by topics, are available as a checklist you can add your own ideas to. This list is a summary for reference. The ideas are explained more fully throughout this book. Download a sample list of 101 marketing actions at: https://craftmarketer.com/book-resources/

BIZ STARTUP
- Choose a catchy business name
- Register for a business license
- Get set up to accept credit cards
- Set up business checking account

PRE-MARKETING
- Write your artist's story
- Design logo
- Draft an elevator pitch
- Choose fonts and colors to match your personal brand
- Add your contact info
- Get business cards designed and printed
- Get hangtags designed and printed
- Get Thank you cards designed and printed
- Record a voice mail message sending people to your website for more info.
- Brand all stationery, like receipts, letterheads, emails, newsletters, etc.

PHOTOS & VIDEOS
- Take lots of attractive photos
- Make product images with white background
- Make how-it's-made images & videos
- Make how-it's-used images & videos
- Make lifestyle images
- Get head shot images of you
- Make behind-the-scenes videos

PRICING
- Research average prices for similar work to yours
- Figure your production cost
- Determine your profit margin

SEO - SEARCH ENGINE OPTIMIZATION
- Use EtsyRank or MerchantWords to find buyer keywords
- Use keywords in social posts
- Use keywords in product listings
- Get inbound links

SELL ON ETSY
- Set up new Etsy shop, or
- Get critiques of your current Etsy shop and adjust accordingly
- List new products or copy product listings using unique keyword-rich titles
- Place keywords in title, tags, descriptions
- Add 10 images per listing
- Connect your Etsy store to your social media
- Test Etsy Ads
- Increase listings regularly
- Market your Etsy store offline
- Offer free shipping if possible

ALTERNATIVES TO ETSY
- List on Amazon Handmade
- List on other Etsy alternatives
- Set up your own domain site
- Add the free WordPress plugin for Etsy Shops

BLOGGING
- Set up a blog about your niche
- Optimize blog posts for SEO
- Syndicate posts to social media

SOCIAL MEDIA
- Post at least once a day or more
- Post with video for engagement
- Post to educate, entertain, inspire
- Post links to your products

- Schedule posting using apps
- Research popular hashtags
- Post on Facebook
- Post to Instagram
- Tweet to Twitter
- Pin to Pinterest boards
- Get social followers' e-mails

SELL WHOLESALE
- Determine production capacity
- Costs = 25% or less of the retail price
- Create a professional presentation
- List on Faire, Tundra, Indieme, WholesaleInABox
- Offer online ordering for stores

LEVERAGE INFLUENCERS' AUDIENCES
- Prepare online media kit
- Identify influencers with Heepsy
- Use Twitter to find reporters
- USNPL lists newspaper writers
- Create brief pitch to media

CUSTOMER MAILING LIST
- Set up e-mail management app like Aweber or Mailchimp
- Ask customers to give e-mail
- Schedule follow-up calendar

PAID ADVERTISING
- Set your daily ad budget
- Start ad campaigns on Etsy, Amazon Handmade, etc.
- Track and measure profits after ad spend
- Adjust ad spend higher when justified
- Adjust ad spend or eliminate poor performing ads

MISCELLANEOUS
- Track and measure all actions
- Listen to what shoppers tell you
- Answer all inquiries quickly
- Personalize communications
- Treat customers fabulously
- Make stuff you love making
- Daily Planner / Marketing Calendar

After you identify which action steps you want to work with, use a calendar to organize and schedule them. A daily planner / marketing calendar protects you from getting lost by mapping the actions you will take over the coming weeks.

Your calendar helps you avoid costly shotgun marketing, and instead, laser-focus on profitable actions you can track and measure.

Now that you have a marketing plan and a calendar of steps to take, one of your early priorities should be researching and strategically placing words and phrases used online by buyers of items similar to yours. This process is called SEO or Search Engine Optimization, outlined in the next chapter.

Chapter 6

SEO, How to Harness Search Engine Traffic

S EO—or search engine optimization—refers to using techniques to improve a web page's likelihood of showing up in search results for specific search terms or keywords. There aren't many ways to market for free, but getting your product listing to show up on Etsy, Amazon, or Google when buyers type in search terms is probably the closest to free you will find.

The factors that go into how e-commerce search engines like Etsy and Amazon rank one page over another for specific keyword searches change and evolve regularly. But there are elements that consistently influence search rankings, which you will discover in the following topics:

- Finding search terms buyers use
- Inbound links to your pages
- Where to place keywords and tags

Search is powerful. It has driven the boom of e-commerce both through computers and more and more on mobile devices. Eighty-seven percent of people using a smartphone search online at least once a day.

People search online for solutions to their problems. They search for opportunities. They search for entertainment. They search to learn. More important to you, they search for handmade products to buy.

Finding Search Terms Buyers Use

When we talk about tags, keywords, and search terms, they refer to the same thing. They are the words and phrases people type in a search bar to find what they need online.

In order for your product pages to show up in search results, you must include popular and relevant search terms used by shoppers. If you don't use popular search terms on your pages, your items won't get found through search.

There are several ways to learn which keywords buyers use. The first way is free, but time-consuming. Go to Etsy, Amazon Handmade, or other online marketplace. Begin typing words that describe a product like yours into the search bar. Most sites will auto-complete your phrase after you type in the first four or five letters, or display a drop-down box with suggestions.

Though you cannot copy and paste those suggestions, you can type them into a list. The drop-down of suggested keywords come from previous buyer searches that resulted in a sale, so they are the exact phrases you want to use in your listings.

You can also get these buyer phrases and a lot more much faster by using a keyword research tool. The most popular and useful apps for handmade sellers:

- EtsyRank.com (for Etsy, limited free plan, basic account around $10 per month)
- MerchantWords.com (for Amazon, basic account around $29 per month)
- Ubersuggest.com (for Google searches, basic account around $10 per month)

If you are just starting your business and on a limited budget, you can subscribe for one month and then cancel. During your month, use the tools as much as you can to accumulate a list of keywords and other data related to your products. When you are ready to expand your product line, come back to the tool to get ideas based on shopper data.

For an example, below are results from research done using EtsyRank. Let's say you make and sell earrings from upcycled, scrap materials. You are not sure about how buyers search for items like yours, so you start your keyword research with "sustainable jewelry." Typing in "sustainable jewelry" in EtsyRank's keyword tool, we see:

sustainable – 2,477 searches on Etsy
sustainable fashion – 78   "
sustainable jewelry – 102   "
sustainable clothing – 559   "

EtsyRank shows terms related to "sustainable" to explore. Let's try some other phrases and see what shows up:

upcycled – 4,060
upcycled clothing – 1,021
upcycled earrings – 618

recycled – 588
recycled earrings – 316
recycled jewelry – 142
recycled materials – 160

eco-friendly – 2,570
eco-friendly jewelry – 128
eco-friendly gift – 104

While "sustainable jewelry" got 102 searches in a recent month, other related search terms were more popular among searchers. That tells us you will get even more visitors by using the new keywords.

One tactic for making use of this is to copy an existing Etsy listing, but alter the title and add a tag that begins with other popular search terms. Using this tactic on my listings, doubled my visitor traffic and sales. More on Etsy tactics in Chapter 7.

Researching product search terms is the place to start optimizing your product listings. But you can also discover more generic search phrases like "gift for her," "father's day gift," or "gift for mom."

If you make items tied to holidays or special times of the year, get your product listings optimized with seasonal phrases a couple of months before the occasion in order for Etsy or Amazon to index your pages.

The broader and shorter the search term, the more difficult it is to rank for. Shoppers use long tail (multi keyword) phrases when they are ready to buy.

For example, "tote bag" is a popular search term (over 90,000 searches on Google in a recent month) but not necessarily one used by shoppers alone.

Whereas, "black tote bag" (8,100 searches in the same recent month) is more specific and probably used by those shopping for exactly that.

Note about using Ubersuggest or other tools based on Google search results data: Google search results data is compiled from many types of inquiries, not all of them from buyers. Ubersuggest is included as a tool here because it can be helpful when creating blog posts for your own website or posts on social media that you want to rank high in Google searches.

Etsy Search Analytics

If you have an Etsy store that has made sales over several months, Etsy provides free "Search Analytics." This is invaluable for Etsy sellers with a sales history. This tool tells you which keyword searches got your product pages showing up in search and resulted in sales. When I analyzed my visitor behavior for the last year, I found search phrases I had not optimized for, but that led to sales. When I created new listings using those phrases, sales increased. To view this tool, go to your Etsy Shop Manager > Marketing > Search analytics.

Inbound Links to Your Pages

Using popular keywords is an important part of SEO for Etsy, Amazon, and other online stores. But there's another element that can affect your ranking in Google, Yahoo, and Bing search results—inbound links pointing to your product listing pages. An example of an inbound link: a blogger writes a review about one of your products and includes a link to your Etsy store.

Inbound links add authority to your page rankings because they are like votes coming in to tell the search engine that your page is relevant for the text in the link.

If you wanted to rank higher for "recycled vintage earrings" in Google searches, you would ask some sites to link to you with the link text reading "recycled vintage earrings." The actual hyperlink that leads to your page become visible when a visitor mouses over the link text.

But you have to be careful not to go overboard with getting too many inbound links saying the same thing. Google sees this as spam. The best SEO practice is to aim for a variety of inbound link texts as it looks more natural to Google. Some inbound link texts could be your URL. Some could be the phrase for which you want to rank high. And others could be semantically-related phrases or your business name.

The fewer competitors there are for a particular phrase, the easier it will be for you to get a top ranking position in search results. However, it can help your pages to include words and phrases related to your subject in your content, even if those phrases are highly competitive and perhaps more generic than your tags.

Though your main keywords should be phrases used by buyers, there is an overall SEO benefit to including a mix of both broad and specific search terms in your product description.

Where to Place Keywords and Tags

Here are the areas where you can make use of tags in your product listings for SEO purposes:

- **Title**: The first 30 characters (first few words) of your title are the most important for SEO, so include the most popular buyer keywords at the beginning.
- **Description**: Create a product description that promises benefits to the buyer. Insert popular keywords and tags throughout.
- **Attributes**: Attributes are extra tags like colors and materials. People search for "red" scarves or "cotton" clothing.
- **"About" page**: Your artist's story is an often-overlooked area to include your keywords. Weave them into your personal narrative.
- **Shop announcement**: Yet another area where you can include popular search terms.
- **Tags**: Use all allowable tags. They should differ from each other. Optimally, tags should match as many of the words in your product's title as possible.
- **Categories**: Categories act like tags, so choose categories relevant to your product line. But if you sell scarves under the category "Scarves" don't waste one of your tags with the word "scarves."
- **Shop policies and terms**: Include your popular search terms in your policies content. Though this area isn't important for Etsy search results, the content on these pages gets read by Google and may appear in their search results.

Engagement

Another factor that influences your website's SEO rankings is the amount and frequency of engagement your pages receive from real people. For example, you post a video on your Facebook page with a link to your website or Etsy store. Your followers click through your link and check out your product pages. That engagement, including how much time a visitor spends on your pages, is tracked and measured by Google, which then becomes part of the algorithm that determines how Google ranks your pages for search terms.

Seasonal SEO

With a basic knowledge of SEO, you can take advantage of seasonal searches. For instance, shoppers search for "Christmas gifts for men" or "girlfriend gifts for Valentines" in the weeks and months leading up to those shopping times.

Change your tags on your product listings throughout the year to position your products for those special occasions. Start using seasonal tags at least two months in advance to give search engines like Google time to index your listings.

Let's put your new SEO knowledge to work. The coming chapters dive deeper into the most popular online marketplaces for handmade products. Though SEO is important, it's one of several elements that makes for a successful e-commerce presence. Etsy is the first place to start as it's inexpensive to sell through, has a vast audience, and is easy to get started with.

Chapter 7

Selling on Etsy

The easiest starting point for selling handmade online is opening or improving an Etsy shop. Their customer base is enthusiastically pro-handmade.

If you follow the advice in this guide, you will be ahead of the pack. Statistically, most would-be sellers don't do well with their Etsy shops. They throw up a few listings without attention to all the moving parts that make a shop profitable and expect buyers to flood in. You'll see their complaints in social media: "Etsy doesn't work!"

Etsy does work, but only when you work at it, and you need patience to see results.

Think of optimizing an Etsy shop as a boot camp training in e-commerce. When you have sales coming from your Etsy store, it is much easier to get results on other platforms like Amazon Handmade, Facebook Shops, and having your own website.

Though Etsy has a lot going for it, there are pros and cons:

Pros

- Immense market of loyal shoppers. Over 46 million users (2019) with gross annual sales of almost $5 billion and growing. Over 80 percent of Etsy purchases come from repeat buyers.
- More than 95% of Etsy sellers work from home.
- Easy to get started for new sellers to set up a shop and add product listings. Etsy provides a Seller Guide at etsy.com/seller-handbook to get you up and running using best practices from successful sellers. YouTube is another source of help with hundreds of free tutorial videos on all aspects of setting up an Etsy store.

- Compared to Amazon Handmade, Etsy seller fees are lower at 5% per sale compared to Amazon's 15% fee.
- Lots of ways to optimize listings for SEO.
- Many Etsy sellers also buy from other sellers to support the handmade lifestyle.

Cons
- Lots of competition, though this chapter's tips can overcome that by helping your listings stand out.
- Etsy takes work and patience to see results.
- The more you sell, the more fees eat into your profits. Each new or renewed listing costs you $.20.
- Etsy gives SEO advantage to sellers who offer free shipping. If your profit margins aren't large enough to provide free shipping, your listings may show up lower in search.
- Almost no control over Etsy ads other than a daily budget and which of your listings get promoted.
- If you don't optimize (SEO) your listings, you have little chance of getting visitors.
- Pricing can become an issue among similar product sellers. You don't want to be in a race to the bottom.
- You can't collect and don't own your customer contact information, though there are ways around that.
- Negative online chatter from whiners and complainers can infect you with negative bias. Etsy is a business; adapt or forget it.

The best practices outlined in this chapter will help you set up your Etsy shop to succeed. Here you will learn about:
- Setup steps
- Images and videos
- Etsy SEO
- Your product descriptions
- Share on social media
- How to treat customers

- Market your Etsy store offline
- If sales are poor

Setup Steps

- Start out by choosing a shop name. To create online branding, use the same name across all your social profiles. Your shop name shows up in your Etsy shop URL. Example: https://www.etsy.com/shop/YourBizName.
- Decide what you will sell and make a list of your products. For ideas, review the keyword research tools in the previous chapter to discover products in demand.
- Read and follow all the guidelines and policies when setting up your shop.
- Add your artist's story to your Seller's Bio. Shoppers want to know about your creative journey making crafts.
- Your "Shop Announcement" gives you a place to add interesting details about your products and your creative process. It is also an overlooked area for placing popular keyword phrases used by Etsy shoppers.
- Design and upload a shop icon, profile image of yourself and (optional) store banner.
- Write a welcome message. If natural, weave in popular search terms. They won't help you with Etsy search rankings, but will help you get found by Google.
- Create your Payment, Shipping, Refund, Seller, and Additional Information policies. Don't omit these as Etsy search favors shops with completed policies.
- Product listings are pages that display information to viewers about your product. Listings include images, a title, a product description, tags, price, shipping, quantity, and materials.
- When setting up a product listing, fill in each section. Each of the areas on the listing page provides another opportunity to appear in searches.
- If you have customer reviews, include them in your

product listing description. Even though viewers can access your reviews elsewhere, repeating one or more of the best ones in the description adds social proof that your product is worth buying.

Images and Videos

Images play a major role when online shoppers browse your listings. Ninety percent of shoppers report that great photos played a part in their buying decision. Take photos of an item from different angles. Include images of people using your item and images of the product with a plain white background. See Chapter 3 for more on photography.

In 2020, Etsy allowed sellers to upload videos for each product listing. According to Unbounce.com, adding video to your pages can increase your conversion rate by up to 80%.

Etsy SEO

In the last chapter, you learned the basics of SEO. You learned how to use keyword data tools like EtsyRank.com to discover keyword search terms used by buyers looking for handmade products.

Here we look at SEO tips specifically to help your Etsy shop listings get found more often in searches. These tactics also help your Etsy pages show up in Google search results.

- Etsy's search engine reads your product titles, tags, categories, and attributes to find search terms matching what buyers are looking for. Therefore, those areas are key for placing or matching popular search terms. For example, if you sold men's scarves, the phrase "mens scarf" should appear in your title, as one of your tags, and in your description. When setting up a men's scarf listing, you would choose the broad category "Scarves."
- Notice that in the above example, I made slight changes from my original item; altering "men's scarves" to "mens

scarf." That's because EtsyRank revealed that the popular search term is spelled "mens scarf."

- Further down on a product listing page, you have an option to create sections in your store. Using the above example, you would create a section called "Mens Scarf" and assign it whenever you list a new men's scarf.
- As mentioned earlier, the most important area of a product listing's title is the first 30 characters. Place your most popular phrases at the beginning of your product listing title. Continuing with our example, a new item listing for a knitted black men's scarf might be titled: "Mens Scarf, Black Mens Scarf, Mens Knit Scarf, Gift for Men"
- Etsy allows you thirteen keyword tags for each listing. Use all of them. As much as possible, your listing's title should match your tags. Tags for the men's black scarf item would include "mens scarf" "black mens scarf" "mens knit scarf" "gift for men" and other related search terms. Note that the tags match the words in the title.
- Include synonyms and semantically related search terms in your product listing titles, tags, and descriptions. For our example, we might also include the tags: "winter scarf" "unisex scarf" and "man scarf" as they show up on EtsyRank's keyword report as popular search terms. Related terms to research: "mens accessories" "mens clothing" "neckware."
- Popular search terms used in your listing titles, tags, and descriptions can also be worked into other areas of your store like your story, shop policies, and announcements.
- Shops with only a few items in a category rank lower in search compared to shops with many listings in the same category.
- Add new item listings to your Etsy store regularly, but not all at once. Aim for a minimum of fifty to a hundred listings. Each listing is a new opportunity to show up in Etsy searches, especially if you use unique keywords and tags in each listing. Etsy gives new listings a slight

boost in search results temporarily to get them going.

- As described earlier, you can copy an existing Etsy listing and alter the title and tags. For example, for a listing for a knitted, black men's scarf, you would have one listing title that begins with "Mens Scarf," a separate listing with a title beginning with "Black Mens Scarf," and another listing with a title starting with "Mens Knit Scarf." Now you have tripled your chances of being found in search results. You have three listings, each optimized for a separate keyword phrase. Note: if you create three listings for basically the same item, have three black scarves on hand or be able to make them fast should you get orders from all the listings on the same day.

- Mentioned before, Etsy sellers with a sales history can take advantage of Etsy's "Search analytics" to learn which search terms buyers used to find your product. Access it through Shop Manager > Marketing > Search analytics. It's not so useful for new sellers because there isn't much traffic or sales to analyze. But if you have been on Etsy awhile and made sales, the search analytics tool will tell you which search words shoppers used to find your items converted to sales.

Product Descriptions

In your product descriptions, tell the customer how your item will transform their life. Features need to be there, but transformations sell. How will your product make their life easier?

Spell-check your listings before posting. When shoppers see misspelled words or grammatical errors, they may imagine your item is as carelessly assembled as your text.

Add a shipping profile or select a shipping profile you want to update. Fill out the shipping profile.

Select your order processing time (how long it will take to ship your order). The shorter the processing time, the more you will convert visitors to customers.

See Appendix 1 for more about creating product descriptions that sell.

Share on Social Media

After you have posted your listings, share them on social. Etsy makes it easy for you to share your product listings, five-star reviews, items that have been recently favorited, and special sales to your social profiles on Pinterest, Facebook, Instagram, and Twitter.

To make use of this feature, go to your Shop Manager > Marketing > Social Media and then look for the tab near the top that reads, "Social accounts." From there, connect your other social profiles. After you have connected your social profiles to Etsy, you are ready to post. Look for and click on the "+Create Post" button. Then Etsy walks you through creating and sharing a post to all your sites. Etsy's tool is free.

If posting frequently is taking too much of your time, schedule your social sharing with tools (subscriptions) like Buffer.com, Hootsuite.com or Tailwindapp.com.

How to Treat Customers

- Etsy has instant messaging that lets you quickly reply to customer inquiries.
- When someone messages you through Etsy, get back with the person as soon as possible. Your fast response builds goodwill.
- Etsy notifies you when a customer leaves a review, favorites an item, or leaves shop feedback. When I get a notification of a review, I send the person a message right away thanking them for taking time to leave a review as it really helps small businesses like mine.
- You can build rapport with customers by engaging through messaging. If I see that a shopper or customer's address is in a city I'm familiar with, I'll mention a restaurant

or annual event I liked and ask them if they know of it. These tiny dialogues have helped build repeat business that would not have happened without the personal interactions.

- Another way to automate building customer relationships is to create a discount coupon for the next purchase. You have the option to set it to go to every customer upon checkout. Go to Shop Manager > Marketing > Sales and Coupons.

- If you get complaints, offer to replace the problem item or issue a refund. Put the customer in control. Don't make them feel they are wrong.

- Just fix problems, even if doing so costs you extra. You've heard the saying, "the customer is always right." It has never been truer than with online sales.

- If you receive a negative review, get in touch with the customer and take care of any issues. After you have made things right, ask the disgruntled shopper to alter their negative rating. Offer a refund or substantial discount coupon if it means getting better feedback.

- Print and include a packing slip that Etsy creates for each order so customers know where the product is coming from. I write on it a big "Thank You" with the person's name at the top.

- Let shoppers know when they can expect their order to ship and make it as soon as you confidently can. Click Shop Manager > Settings > Shipping settings.

If Sales Are Poor

- If your Etsy shop has been up for a while but is performing poorly, hire successful Etsy sellers to critique it. Shop reviews cost anywhere from $20 to $100 or more. Fiverr. com provides Etsy shop critiques cheaper than those offered on Etsy. But only work with Fiverr providers who have all five-star reviews. I bought Etsy shop reviews from three different Fiverr providers, because I wanted a variety of perspectives of my shop. You might think all of them would offer the same suggestions. Though on some points they agreed, each of the reviewers gave unique ideas that helped my sales after I put them into practice.

- Review your product listing descriptions. See Appendix 1.
- Browse the community forums and teams (groups) on Etsy to learn and share experiences with other craft artists about setting up, marketing, and running an Etsy store.
- Try listing more items. Increasing the number of your product listings can boost your sales. You'll have more pages through which shoppers can find you. And Etsy search appears to favor shops that have more items than other sellers in the same category.
- Run discount coupons for key shopping dates. Etsy provides you with a calendar of peak buying seasons with tips for tying in special offers. Go to Shop Manager > Marketing > Key shopping dates.
- Boost sales by offering free shipping, if your profit margin allows it. Etsy created a seller option called Guaranteed Free Shipping for orders over $35. Sellers who opt in to the program get priority in search results over sellers who do not offer free shipping. You can also go into your Shop Manager > Marketing > Sales and coupons. By using Etsy's free shipping coupon (choose "no end date"), Etsy displays a free shipping badge on your shop's product pages. If you set up free shipping as a shipping option, you won't get the Etsy badge. The Etsy badge helps your listings show up better in search results. Even if you have to raise your prices to cover shipping, it will increase your visits and sales.

Shopping blogs and social media influencers seek new products to review. But the competition for getting reviews can be tough. Magazines, newspapers, and freelance writers also report on handmade products they think will interest their readers. See Chapter 17 for how to get publicity from influencers.

One of the advantages of working with Etsy is the company's commitment to making sellers successful. In addition to marketing the Etsy platform to consumers, Etsy integrates with other platforms to help you run your shop better. See https://etsyapps.com/

When you get sales from your Etsy listings, consider scaling up your business with Etsy Ads, as described in Chapter 18.

Etsy is great for learning how to set up and promote an e-commerce site for your handmade fashion crafts. After you make sales on Etsy, consider expanding onto the giant e-commerce platform, Handmade on Amazon.

Chapter 8

Selling on Amazon Handmade

Eyeing Etsy's success, Amazon Handmade opened in 2015. Reviews by maker-sellers have been mixed. Those who have done well report better sales than Etsy. Others say Etsy is a better market for them. You can't know how your products will do until you try them on Amazon. One thing is certain, Amazon has a huge marketplace of buyers.

As a seller on Amazon Handmade, you get:

- Access to the world's largest online marketplace of buyers.
- Amazon check out is trusted by users.
- Amazon's Seller Central dashboard from where you can run sales reports that show impressions, click-throughs, and sales.
- Robust ad campaign manager.
- Advanced seller apps reveal exact search terms used by Amazon buyers of products like yours.
- Product listings can be tweaked for better SEO performance.

However, you also have:

- Lots of competition, even in the handmade category.
- Set up is more complex compared to Etsy
- Amazon Handmade takes work and patience to see results.
- Amazon takes 15% of every sale as opposed to Etsy's 5% commission.

Setting Up to Sell on Amazon

Before you apply to sell on Amazon Handmade, first make sure your product is in one of their approved categories.

Applying and getting set up as a seller on Amazon Handmade is not as simple and fast as other online marketplaces for handmade products. Amazon requires proof of identity from sellers.

Unlike Etsy, you cannot just open a shop and start uploading product listings. Some applicants have reported waiting several weeks or longer for approval. The application link is: https://services.amazon.com/handmade/handmade.html.

If accepted, you must subscribe to Amazon's Professional Account for sellers. The monthly charge of $40 is currently waived for Handmade sellers, but that could change by the time you read this book.

Amazon Handmade gives you an Artisan's Profile, where you can post your artist's story and upload images of yourself. This is the place to share how you came to be a maker, your creative process, interesting facts about what you do, and more.

Setting up product page listings one at a time is straightforward but tedious. Copy and paste the content you used on your Etsy listings section by section, but it is time-consuming.

For examples of product listings on Amazon Handmade that do a good job of selling, browse the Amazon Handmade bestsellers. Amazon shows you the top sellers and you can drill down into categories to find products like yours. Click through to view the top selling products' listings.

Make your product listing descriptions human-friendly, while including popular search terms. See Appendix 1.

Unlike on Etsy, you cannot create sections within your Amazon Handmade shop. Your product listings show up in the order that you publish them.

Amazon Handmade allows for product personalizing if you offer that. When setting up a product, you can add extra custom options for customers to fill in.

Also see the Amazon Handmade Seller Resource Guide at http://go.amazonsellerservices.com/resourceguide

Offering Free Shipping via FBA

Amazon Prime members get free shipping and buy more often than non-members. I've tested listing products where I do the shipping and where FBA (Fulfilled By Amazon) does shipping, and sales were much better working with FBA.

FBA will only work for you if your profit margin covers your added costs. Through fBA, you ship (at your expense) your products to Amazon warehouses. They fulfill orders to their more than ninety million Amazon Prime member buyers. FBA charges you an additional shipping fee for every sale.

If you aren't sure if your profit margin is enough to work with FBA, use the free profit calculator at: https://salecalc.com/amazon

With 85% of Amazon shoppers reporting they hesitate to make a purchase because of shipping charges, offering free shipping sets you apart from most handmade sellers.

Amazon SEO

SEO is the top factor in getting views from Amazon's huge marketplace of shoppers. If you don't use keywords used by shoppers, your listings won't get found in search results.

To see how search on Amazon works, go to the Amazon Handmade category and start typing in words that describe your product. Amazon will start to auto-populate your search with suggested keywords. Those suggested words come from shopper searches that have resulted in sales.

MerchantWords.com helps you quickly discover more buyer search terms than you can find on your own. Starting from your own list of words and phrases, MerchantWords delivers a list of keywords you may not have thought of. You'll also see how strong the competition is for your products. The service costs

$29 a month, but if you only have a few items to research, you could subscribe for one month and then cancel.

- Place the most popular keywords at the beginning of your title and your product descriptions.
- Amazon allows for additional keywords—similar to Etsy tags—in each listing.
- Blend popular keywords into readable copy that's interesting to people looking for products like yours.

Make customer service your top priority. Amazon shoppers look at reviews before making purchases. Double-check your product and packaging quality before shipping. Be willing to refund an unhappy customer.

Your profit margins will be lower on Amazon than most other online marketplaces because of their higher seller fees. If you can afford the lower margins, selling more products may be worth the efforts.

After you have seen your product listings on Amazon convert shoppers to buyers, Amazon offers a robust ad manager for scaling up your sales. To learn more about Amazon ads, see Chapter 18.

The next chapter explains how to sell handmade items on eBay. It may surprise you to learn that many handmade sellers use eBay to expand their sales.

Chapter 9

Selling on eBay

D o you know which platform makers sold their items online from before Etsy started in 2005? It was eBay. Though eBay is more often thought of for buying and selling bargains, makers and artisans sell their work from this platform every day.

For instance, in a 30-day period (data from June, 2020) the following number of handmade items successfully sold on eBay containing the search terms:

- handmade soap: 3,447
- handmade jewelry: 8,066
- handmade knife: 39,134
- handmade quilts:5,732
- handmade wooden box: 827
- A search for the word "handmade" with the filters, "New," "Sold," and "US Only" brought back 821,180 product listings.

To research the market for items like yours. Go to eBay. com. In the search bar, type in your item's most popular key-word phrase gathered from the research you did in Chapter 6. Then, go to the left menu bar on the search results page. Check boxes for "New," "Sold Items," and other filters you want. You may want to view only items from US sellers. If so, check the box "US Only." You can also filter results to only include "Buy It Now" listings and not "Auctions." Ebay will show you new items like yours that sold from "Buy It Now" listings in a recent month from US sellers.

After you have a search results page for items like yours, browse the listings. Note the prices, images, listing titles, and descriptions. You don't have to reinvent the wheel, you can create your own version of winning listings. You don't want to copy other listings, as it violates copyright, and eBay will reject duplicate listings.

Another benefit from this kind of research is that it reveals what shoppers will pay for items like yours. How do these prices match with yours? Would you make a profit selling your products on eBay at the average selling price of items like yours?

Power Seller Tips

Successful eBay sellers share common practices including:
- Look at "sold" item listings as models for pricing, images, and writing descriptions. Follow the directions above for researching "sold" items like yours.
- Use SEO when writing your titles and descriptions. See Chapter 6 for researching popular keywords.
- Use the best images possible. Take photos of your item from different angles. Include lifestyle images of people using your product. See Chapter 3 for tips on creating better photos.
- Create new listings regularly instead of all on the same day, because your listings will show up more in search results if you are posting over time.
- Offer 30-day returns to remove the risk to buyers.
- If your profit margins allow it, provide free shipping. Free shipping is a major conversion factor.
- Ask for a review after a customer has received their item.
- Generate trust using the following guidelines.

Aim for Positive Feedback

eBay provides user feedback ratings for buyers and sellers. Feedback ratings, positive ones that is, are the most important way of conveying trust to the potential customers who don't know you.

When browsing auction listings on eBay, buyers take into consideration your feedback rating before placing a bid.

When a seller has negative feedback, an experienced buyer won't bid. Therefore, it is important that you make it a priority to always follow up with customer inquiries and provide prompt delivery to elicit the highest feedback ratings you can. Whenever you have occasion to be in contact with a customer during the fulfillment process, always be courteous and respectful to insure you get the best ratings.

In your listings:

- Be completely honest about your item.
- Ask bidders to be certain the item is what they want before placing a bid.
- Be prompt, polite and friendly when responding to even dumb questions, which you will receive by email.
- Describe your crafting process to give shoppers an appreciation of what goes into each piece. Spell it out that your item is handmade.
- List any defects, scuffs, or scratches, even small ones.
- If you are selling items made of fabric, let bidders know if they are from a smoke-free and pet-free home.
- Include exact measurements, weights and other qualifying descriptions of your items.
- Invite inquiries from bidders who may want additional information and assurances.
- Put a notice on your listings asking bidders to please read your payment and shipping terms before they place a bid.
- Specify whether you will ship internationally.
- Check out a bidder's Feedback Rating. If they have negative feedback, you can tell them politely, you don't deal with users with lower than a certain rating. Also include it on your 'About Me' page and on your auction descriptions.

eBay Fees

Fees for selling on eBay change. Commission varies if you are selling one or two items or selling from your own eBay store. See eBay's fee page at https://www.ebay.com/help/selling/fees-credits-invoices/selling-fees?id=4364

The monthly fee for an eBay store starts at $7.95 a month and goes up according to how many listings and other features you want.

eBay Selling Tools

Selling apps help you research, create listing templates, bulk upload, and manage your eBay listings. Use eBay's free Selling Manager and test your listings. If selling your items on eBay is profitable and you want to scale up your sales on the platform, check out the paid app services. Some tools offer a month's free trial:

- https://www.ebay.com/help/selling/selling-tools/selling-manager-selling-manager-pro?id=4098 (Selling Manager is free from eBay)
- http://www.inkfrog.com (subscription service)
- https://www.vendio.com (subscription service)
- https://www.3dsellers.com (subscription service_
- https://www.sellbrite.com (subscription service)

See more resources for eBay sellers at: https://www.ebay.com/help/selling#ebay-tools

After sales come in from Etsy, Amazon, or eBay, you may be thinking about expanding. You need a central hub, your own website, from which you can link to your sales channels, social media profiles, and collect contact information to build a customer mailing list. Let's look at the easiest, fastest, and cheapest ways to set up your own website next.

Chapter 10

Selling from Your Own Website

If you spend time on Facebook, Instagram, or Pinterest, you may have accumulated a following. But those followers belong to the platform, not you. Unless you can get them to join your mailing list, there's always the risk of losing them should your account get closed or something happens to the platform. A website of your own lets you offer a newsletter and build a list of loyal customers.

Having your own website offers many other advantages:

- Your website can act as a hub from which you link to your social media profiles, product listing pages, and your "About the Artist" page or media kit.
- Having your own domain name promotes your brand.
- You don't pay commissions for sales coming through your own site, only credit card transaction fees.
- With your own site, you have creative control over how it looks. You can change the layout and design and add as many pages as you like.
- Your images, descriptions and other information are not on another site that could close your account at their own discretion or go out of business.
- Other sites contain vast amounts of data that may have no relevance to your craft products. With your own site, you create content that focused around your subject and therefore more likely to rank high for your keywords in search results.

- Your custom domain name makes it easier to be found for your business name in search engine results.
- You can accumulate incoming links which help your rankings in the search engines.
- With your own domain name, you can create professional appearing e-mail addresses for increasing trust and name recognition like: shelly@shellyshandmades.com.
- By registering a domain name related to your business, you prevent others from using that name. See Chapter 1.
- Many hosting services now offer easy set up for installing software like Wordpress so you can quickly install and operate your own blog and take in e-commerce orders.
- You can promote your domain name on your business cards, brochures, and anywhere else. Even if you change web hosts, your domain name remains the same.
- Web hosting is cheap; often less than $10 a month.

Registering a Domain Name

The first step in getting your own website is to register a domain name. There are many domain registrars to choose from. Examples include NameCheap.com and Godaddy.com, and many others.

Your domain name is part of your branding. It should be memorable, easy to spell, and match or closely match your business profile names on Facebook, Instagram, Pinterest, and other social platforms.

Always try to get the .com extension first. People use the .com extension automatically, without thinking about .net, .biz, or any of the other extensions.

Suppose your business name is more than one word, like Jade's Wood Works. You might register Jadeswoodworks.com. But using your personal name, like JadeBartlow.com, allows room for potential future changes outside of woodworking products in your business.

Hosting

When you register a domain name, you need a host, like Hostgator.com, Hostmonster.com, and Bluehost.com. These services all come with lots of features for enhancing your site. As part of the hosting service, they provide easy set up for installing Wordpress.

Hosting plans cost anywhere from $5 to $100 a month depending on the service. For most handmade sellers, the cheapest service will be enough. As your business grows, you can upgrade to a plan that offers more features.

Free Website Hosting

If you are on a tight budget, there are free website hosts for your business site like Wix.com. The attraction is that it's free and easy to set up. However, the features offered are limited. If you are serious about creating a sustainable business, invest in getting your own domain name and a reliable hosting service.

Shopping Cart Options

Many web hosting services provide a free shopping cart module which you can access through your domain name's control panel. However, if you need more features or wish to customize your cart, see these shopping cart providers:

- Shopify.com — Shopify is for small businesses who want to sell products through an online store. Service plans start at around $29 a month. See Chapter 16 for tips on using Shopify.
- PayPal.com — PayPal is used by many of the online auction sites and storefronts, but you can also get a business account and add it's shopping cart features onto your blog or website pages.
- Woocommerce — is a free Wordpress plugin that allows you to take orders and process sales from a website using Wordpress.

Wordpress

Wordpress is arguably the most popular and easiest to use platform for building a website. Youtube offers hundreds of free tutorials on every aspect of using Wordpress and its many free themes and plugins.

Wordpress is SEO-friendly. The free plugin from Yoast, lets you quickly optimize a post to rank better for specific search terms. Yoast scans your blog posts and suggests how many keywords to use, where to place them, how long your content should be, the readability of your content, and more SEO goodies.

The most important places to include popular search keywords are:
- Page title
- Headlines
- Beginning of text
- Links to other pages on your site
- Links to trusted sites
- URL

Mobile Friendly

Most of your visitor traffic and many of your sales will come from shoppers using their mobile device. Fortunately, Website themes are built to be mobile-friendly, so you can design your site knowing it will render well on a smartphone. However, take care to use images that are more "portrait" than "landscape" oriented as wide images will be rendered smaller to accommodate the screen on a cell phone.

Blogging

Adding a blog to your marketing mix allows you to publish articles, images and videos around topics related to your handmade products and grow your e-mail mailing list. Because search engines love new content, blog pages often rank higher in Google search results than static web pages.

Blogging is a way to express yourself without editing, an instant way to get published, a journal from which to sprout product news, and a way to create a community.

It's also a way to attract and stay in touch with new customers. People who read your blog get to know you as a human being rather than a marketer. Eighty-one percent of U.S. online consumers rely on advice from blogs according to Blogher.com.

Each blog post is an article page. The more pages you have on your site, the more opportunities to get found in Google search results.

Blogging Alternatives to Wordpress

If you don't have your own domain site, you can create free blogs on the following sites:
* https://www.blogger.com/
* https://www.tumblr.com/
* https://medium.com/
* https://jekyllrb.com/

Tips for Blog Posting

* Set up categories for your blog posts as it helps you and your readers find organized content. For instance, start a category for "how to use" for posts about how to use products like yours. Another category could be "how to DIY" where visitors can learn to make their own.
* Articles with images and videos of your handmade products get almost 100% more views, so make your posts media-rich.
* For every seven to ten useful content posts, write a post that pitches one of your products like a new product, sale, or event where you'll be displaying.
* WordPress plugins, Zapier.com and IFTTT.com let you automatically syndicate posts and images from your

blogs to multiple social media sites.

- WordPress plugins like Etsy Shop (free) let you connect and display your Etsy shop listings so you don't have to use a separate shopping cart to process transactions.
- Use EtsyRank.com and Ubersuggest to research popular search words and phrases. Place those words and phrases in your blog article's title, URL, content, image file names, and tags.

18 Ways to Inspire Trust on Your Website

Studies show that confidence is the number one factor in influencing a buying decision. It makes sense then to make visitors to your online pages feel that you are trustworthy and safe to do business with. Here are some confidence-building elements to consider including on your Web pages or on sites where you have a storefront:

1. Create a site that is user friendly. Make navigating easy and intuitive.

2. Write in a personal, conversational tone so your visitors will know they are dealing with a real human being.

3. Add new products and content regularly.

4. Proofread all your text and correct typos, misspellings and grammatical errors.

5. State that products are available for immediate shipping.

6. Make your site interactive; allow customers ways to communicate with you through comments.

7. Include real customer testimonials (you will need their permission) and any review quotes you get from publications or the media (you don't need permission to quote the media.)

8. Make your prices easy to see and include any shipping and handling charges up front so customers will know the total they will be paying.

9. Include brilliant photos and videos, and lots of them.

10. Make it clear who owns the site and list several ways of reaching you, like your phone numbers, contact e-mail address,

postal address and alternatives to online ordering. Use an e-mail address from your own domain like jenna@jennaspurses.com.

11. For accepting payments, you will probably accept credit cards and/or PayPal. Include the graphic logos of Mastercard, Visa, Discover, American Express, and PayPal on your Web pages, because they instill trust.

12. Include an alternative order page for those who would rather call, mail or fax in an order.

13. Publish a page with a privacy policy and state that you do not share your visitors contact information with other parties (except credit card companies when a sale is made.)

14. Put a statement on every page that shopping on your site is SSL, safe and secure (assuming that your site has a security certificate.)

15. State a guarantee. Remove the risk of buying and more people will do business with you. If you have a refund policy, be sure to make it known.

16. Check all your links to make sure they work.

17. Avoid linking to sites that have nothing to do with your craft.

18. Offer a customer newsletter for announcing special offers and new products.

Grow Your Customer List

You might think a happy customer would naturally want to contact you the next time they need a memorable gift. The truth is people may never think of you after your first sale, probably because you failed to stay in touch with them.

One survey showed that 68 percent of people who stopped buying from a business were treated with indifference by an employee or the owner.

In the rush toward profits, it's very easy to get caught up in thinking that business is about sales, instead of relationships. But it is more profitable to go after those who know you. The estimated cost for accumulating new customers is around six times higher than the costs to reactivate former buyers.

It helps to feel like you have a good reason to reconnect with past customers. When you know about them, you can personalize future follow-ups to:

- Provide something the customer perceives as beneficial—such as a discount coupon or a new collectible,
- Show you care, because you reached out.
- Make each prospect feel important, not forsaken.

Tools for Capturing E-mails

The following tools help you capture e-mails and manage your mailing list. You can create a newsletter, a series of autoresponders, or send out a special offer or let your customers know about a new product you are launching: Aweber.com, Mailchimp.com, Getresponse.com, and Convertkit.com.

These tools also allow you to personalize e-mails to get a better response. An example is an e-mail addressed to a person by first name in the e-mail subject area and with the person's name included in the body text of the e-mail. One study showed that personalized e-mails generated over 400 percent more sales on average than non-personalized e-mails.

Tracking Your Visitor Statistics

If you have your own website, you can use the free Google Analytics code to track visitors. Google gives you access to your traffic statistics and where they came from. Watch your visitor reports to learn which ads brought clickthroughs and then converted to sales.

Your website can connect to all of your other social profiles. One of your goals should be to use your site to capture emails of your followers on Facebook, Instagram, Pinterest, and anywhere else you post. The next chapter gives you an overview of how social media marketing can work to expand your business.

Chapter 11

Social Media Marketing Overview

Social media offers multiple ways to grow a fan base for your handmade products. Social networking sites can help you gather new leads, increase sales, and follow up with customers. You can:

- Post product images and videos
- Learn what customers think and how they communicate
- Interact with customers to build relationships
- Link more visitors to your Etsy shop or website
- Check out what your competitors are doing to market their things

To help you include social media marketing in your handmade business, this chapter covers:

- Social marketing tips
- Scheduling tools
- Moving followers over to your e-mail list

Social Marketing Tips

Before we go into the major social platforms, the following checklist acts as a primer for social posting:

- Get familiar with how a platform functions. People hang out on social sites for specific reasons. If you learn something that works to promote your Instagram posts, the same tactic may not work on Pinterest or Twitter.

- Some sellers say Instagram sends them more customers. For others, it's Pinterest or Facebook. Which is best for you? Test some product posts and measure your results.
- Post several times a day. Use tools described later in this chapter to schedule post deliverance across sites.
- In your posts, be helpful. Be inspiring. Be entertaining. Be educational.
- Posts with images get more shares on Facebook and the most retweets on Twitter.
- Posts with videos get the most engagement.
- The organic reach of your posts is becoming more limited. To get more viewers, pay for ads as described in Chapter 18.
- Reply to people's comments on your posts. The more engagement you can get happening, the more your posts will show up organically.
- How often should you promote your product when posting socially? Start out with seven posts that help, entertain or educate, and then post your product-related article or link. Repeat a few times and notice how your followers respond.

Social Posts Scheduling Tools

Managing all of your profiles across several sites one at a time can quickly take up your day. In Chapter 7, Selling on Etsy, one of the tools in your Etsy Shop Manager under Marketing is the Social Media option. You can quickly connect and promote posts of your listings, reviews and favorites directly to your Facebook, Instagram, Pinterest, and Twitter profiles.

There are other scheduling tools (paid subscriptions) to help leverage your time. Try one or more for a month (some offer free trials) and then decide if you want to stay with that tool or try a different one.

- Outfy.com
- Hootsuite.com

- Buffer.com
- Tailwindapp.com
- SproutSocial.com

Moving Followers on Your Mailing List

If your favorite social site folds or changes policies, or if your account gets shut down, all of your followers and the work you did to get them vanishes. There is no back-up.

You may not own your social followers, but you do own your mailing list. And that list will be yours to promote through regardless of what happens to your social platforms.

To get your followers to give you their e-mail addresses, offer an incentive like a coupon, free download, a newsletter subscription, or a mini course. See the tools for capturing e-mails mentioned in Chapter 10.

Your e-mail list is an asset. Back it up frequently. Use it to stay in touch with your tribe.

Each social site attracts visitors for specific reasons, so those visitors' behavior patterns and how you market to them needs tailoring. For instance, Facebook fans respond to or engage with posts in one way, fans on Instagram another. Rather than attempt to master all social sites, go for getting results on one or two of the sites you are at ease with before promoting on others.

Shopify and other multichannel listing apps let you quickly list or import your Etsy products to multiple social sites. See Chapter 16 to learn about scaling up your sales through building shops on Facebook, Instagram, and Pinterest.

The next several chapters provide best practices for creating followers and sales on the top social sites for reaching handmade product buyers.

Chapter 12

Facebook Tips

O ver two billion people use Facebook. Almost eighty percent of shoppers in the US have found products to buy while on Facebook. Once you have a personal profile set up on Facebook, you can set up a free Facebook page for your business. Facebook personal profiles are limited to adding 5,000 friends, but Facebook pages can have an unlimited number of likes and followers.

Facebook Shop

Sell directly from your Facebook page by enabling a Facebook Shop tab in your page settings. In 2020, Facebook announced an upgrade to the Shop feature in line with being more competitive with Amazon and other e-commerce sites. Shoppers can browse your items, make a purchase, and pay for it while remaining on your Facebook page.

- Set up a Facebook Catalog inside your Facebook Business Manager: https://business.facebook.com/
- Apps like Shopify help you quickly import your Etsy or other product listing data to your Facebook shop. See Chapter 16.
- You get access to "Insights" providing visitor data you can't get from a profile page. You will learn how many people your posts reached, how many new likes you got, how many people engaged with your posts, and more.
- Getting sales from Facebook means getting visual, big time. Studies show Facebook users respond more to imagery and video than simple text.

- Alternatively, the Shop tab can link to your other website or your Etsy shop. But sending customers away from Facebook creates an added step they have to take and will lower conversion rates.
- To collect payments, set up an account with a payment gateway like Stripe.com. After your payment account is open, add products in your store. For a detailed video on setting up a Facebook Shop, see https://www.youtube.com/watch?v=jahKOMsOka0 .

Posting Tips

- Post consistently, like several times a week.
- Post from your FB Page, not your personal profile.
- Upload images of your products, videos of your creative process and posts with a mix of video, imagery, and text.
- Video rules on Facebook. Facebook Live videos get six times as many interactions as regular videos. FB Live videos also rank higher in newsfeeds.
- Post useful tips related to your products. If you make accessories, offer tips like "5 ways to use this _____ to look great in a hurry while helping the planet."
- Avoid making politically or religiously charged posts.

Facebook Stories

When you post to your FB page in the normal way, that post shows up in some but not all of your viewers' feeds. As a person's feed fills up with incoming posts, your message cycles down in the newsfeed as newer posts appear at the top.

FB stories appear above your users' feed and remain there for 24 hours. If you add to your story several times a day, it keeps your business name in front of your fans instead of it vanishing in the feed.

You can add stories to your FB page from your smartphone. They can include photos, videos, and text.

Stories work best as a "behind the scenes" look into your fashion crafts business. For example, you might shoot a video of you creating a new piece. Or, for fun, completely messing one up.

"Buy Sell" Groups on Facebook

- FB "Buy Sell" groups for handmade products allow you to post images, product descriptions, and links to your item's sales page on Etsy or elsewhere. Buyers join these groups to browse for handmade items. See Facebook.com/groups/craftsu.
- To find groups on FB to post your products in, type "buy sell handmade" or "buy sell crafts" in the search bar at the upper left of any FB page. Then click on the Groups tab to narrow results to only look at Groups.
- Facebook.com/marketplace/ is FB's own buy/sell market. It's used by 800 million people globally each month. Sellers list items for sale. Shoppers browse for bargains. Like with Craigslist, there is no fee to use the marketplace.
- FB Marketplace displays tons of stuff people are looking to get rid of at low prices. Search results are tailored to your local area.
- A search for "handmade" brought up hundreds of items near me. Most of the listings were pre-owned items. Some were new and priced at the same retail price the seller asks on Etsy.
- Though listing handmade products next to used stuff won't set your products apart, your item on FB Marketplace gives you a virtual shopping cart for free. You link directly to your product listing, buyers can pay through Facebook Payments, and you ship the item or deliver it locally.

Chapter 13

Pinterest Tips

Pinterest.com is a visual search engine where you pin your favorite images and videos from across the web. Pins on Pinterest don't expire, so investing time here can pay off in the long term.

The site gets over two billion searches each month. It's considered by many to be the most popular visual search platform. More relevant to sellers, 93% of pinners use Pinterest for planning purchases.

For example, fans of Pinterest use it to search for fashion tips, what's in style, plan weddings, baby arrivals, DIY how-tos, and much more. Fashion and DIY are among the top interests on Pinterest.

The average sale arising from a Pinterest search is close to $60—higher than average sales from Twitter or Facebook buyers.

Pinterest and Etsy

Not everyone who views your pins or follows you on Pinterest will click through to your online store, but enough do to justify investing time building a presence there. Pins don't disappear like Facebook posts. Even when I have neglected pinning for long periods, my Etsy store statistics show visitors checking out my items from Pinterest almost every day. One of my pins from 2012 still sends traffic to my site.

Set Up Business Account

- Choose the Pinterest business account option when registering. It offers more options, including access to Pinterest Analytics, which tracks and measures how engaging your pins are.
- If you already have a personal profile, convert it to a business account for free.
- When setting up your profile, choose the same business name you use across all of your online sites.
- As with every place you sell online, include popular tags/keywords related to your business in your profile description and when naming your boards so you get discovered in searches.
- Go to "Settings" and "Claim." Add your website if you have one. Also, claim your Etsy store, Instagram and YouTube accounts. Claiming your accounts gives you access to Analytics that show how visitors engage with your pins.

Set Up a Pinterest Shop

After you have set up a Pinterest business account and claimed your website, you can set up shopping Pins and catalogs. You can feature up to eight product groups.

Product Pins contain metadata and are formatted to let viewers know that they're shoppable. They contain pricing info, availability, product title and description.

Import a data source of your product listings or use an import app like Shopify or others described in Chapter 16. Working with data feeds can get complicated, if you've never done it. For detailed step-by-step help with setting up products for sale on Pinterest, see https://help.pinterest.com/en/business/article/create-a-shop

Creating Boards

- Pinterest boards let you organize your images by topics. After you have set up your profile, your next step is to create five to ten boards to place your pins in.
- Collect a mix of content browsers will enjoy looking through. For example, if you knit or crochet scarves from sustainable materials, create one board for pins of your scarves, another board with pins teaching people different ways to wear scarves, and another board that shows your scarves worn on special occasions.
- If you don't have a lot of product images of your own to fill in your boards in the beginning, fill them with images of related tips, guides, and products you like.
- Choose a popular keyword tag for the board name. Include a description using several related keywords. Upload an eye-catching cover image. Just as people judge a book by its cover, they explore your pins based on your boards' cover images.
- For examples of how to build out your boards, just search Pinterest using words that describe your products or customers; make a list of the most popular pinners and observe how they've created their boards and pins.

Gathering Followers

- Search for topics related to your products and find the most popular boards. When you find someone with a million or more followers, click the "Followers" link on their profile. A drop-down list appears. Start following the popular pinners' followers that appear to be active on Pinterest.
- Follow up to fifty new people every day. If you have set up your boards with interesting image collections, you will find popular pinners' followers following you.

Pin new images daily as they show up in your new followers' feeds.

- Engage with your followers. Comment on their pins. Create conversations.
- Join Tailwind Tribes. Here you can join groups (tribes) of like-minded people. You share their posts and they share yours. See: https://www.tailwindapp.com/tribes.

Pinning

- Most Pinterest users are female—think of pins that will appeal to women.
- Pin consistently, even daily. Use a scheduling tool to make this easy.
- Pin images and videos. Pin helpful tips.
- Pinterest wants more videos. Videos rank well in search on Pinterest.
- Pinterest favors pins/pinners that get higher engagement with higher search results.
- Pinterest studies reveal that lifestyle images get more attention than product images, 150% more purchases than product photos alone.
- Videos pinned on Pinterest get higher engagement than other sites.
- Optimize pins to get more viewers from search. Each pin can have a description. In the description use popular search terms and tags related to your products. Link directly to your product's listing on Etsy or elsewhere so viewers can click to buy instantly.
- As mentioned earlier, you can pin your Etsy listings, five-star reviews, and more on Pinterest through your Etsy Shop Manager.
- Rich pins are a special format that gives more context around an idea or product by displaying extra information on the pin. Rich pins are free, but your pins have to meet requirements and be approved. The steps for

setting up rich pins are found at: help.pinterest.com/en/business/article/rich-pins.

If you have a business account on Pinterest, you can access paid advertising through Promoted Pins. As with all ad campaigns, set your spending budget at the minimum dollar amounts, and test for two to three weeks. Pinterest provides ad tracking that reveals how many people view your ads, click through, and buy a product, if you are selling directly on Pinterest.

Chapter 14

Instagram Tips

Instagram is a mobile-dominated platform for telling visual stories—98% of Instagram content comes from phones. While Instagram has over a billion users, 59% are under thirty years old. Many Etsy sellers report they get more sales via Instagram than Pinterest or Facebook. Understandable, since over 1,926,000 Instagram users follow Etsy's profile there.

Instagram members have a high engagement rate. Over 70% of users have bought something found there using their mobile phone.

Set Up Business Account

- Download the Instagram app and install on your phone. Set up your new account as a business account, or convert your existing profile to a business one.
- Like with other social sites, a business account allows you to promote or advertise your posts. You also get access to "Insights" (analytics) about your posts, hashtags, visitors, and engagements.
- Choose the same username (or a close variant if taken) that you use on Etsy and all your social media profiles. Upload the same profile image you use on other social sites.
- Include a link to your Etsy or other online shop in your profile.
- An Instagram business account is required to set up Instagram shopping.

Instagram Shopping

Instagram allows shoppable posts which visitors can buy your products by clicking a button. Shoppable posts show a shopping bag icon so viewers know they can purchase directly. Users can also click through to browse your "Shop" catalog from your Instagram profile.

- As Instagram is owned by Facebook, start the set up process on Instagram by first a Facebook Catalog in your Facebook Business Manager.
- Create a Facebook Shop. For a detailed video on setting up a Facebook Shop, see https://www.youtube.com/watch?v=jahKOMsOka0. Or use Shopify or another multichannel listing app. See Chapter 16.
- Connect your Facebook Shop to your Instagram business account.
- Upload images to your Instagram account that you want to tag for sale.
- For a step-by-step walkthrough, see https://www.facebook.com/business/instagram/shopping/guide

Posting Images

- With the app open, take a photo with your phone, write a cute caption, and push "share." You have the option to add image-editing filters before you share your photos.
- The app automatically sizes your uploaded image to display on mobile devices. Horizontal (portrait) oriented images fit the screen well as most people naturally hold their phones horizontally.
- Sharing images comes with options. You can share to your other social media profiles. You can add hashtags. You can tag other people in the image. And you can add your location so viewers will know where the image was taken.

- You can also upload images from your computer.
- In your post you can add a brief caption. Caption text can show up in search results, so include relevant hashtags.

Videos

- Instagram lets you add and edit videos up to sixty seconds long. Videos can come directly from your phone or from content you have transferred to your phone from another source.
- Sellers can add a call to action at the end of a video.

Instagram Stories

- Instagram stories, like FB stories, feature your photos and videos at the top of your follower's feeds. They remain there for twenty-four hours.
- Upload your story-behind-the-scenes of your handmade gig. Post stories about how you got started in your fashion crafts business, how you make your products, and what inspires you.
- Use the "poll" feature to ask your followers questions. Discover what they think about your stories.

Hashtags

- Hashtags are mashed-up phrases preceded by the # sign. Example: #handmadewedding. The # sign turns the phrase into a clickable link. Hashtags help your posts get found in search.
- Hashtags can help you uncover other sellers with products like yours.
- Multi-worded hashtags help you attract buyers instead of just researchers. If you make and sell wedding items, broad topic hashtags like #weddings won't be as useful

to you as more specific hashtags like #weddingfashions, or #handmadeweddings.

- You can add up to thirty hashtags when you post or comment, but adding so many looks spammy. The fix is to add a comment and include hashtags in the comment.
- Studies show posts with multiple hashtags get twice the amount of interaction with viewers.
- Mix your choice of hashtags among your posts and comments.
- Use one of your hashtags for your Instagram name.
- Look at the posts on the most popular profiles in your niche. See hashtags you had not thought of?
- After your profile has received likes, comments, and followers over time use the "Insights" feature in your business account to discover which hashtags brought the most traffic to your Etsy store or website.
- Find keywords by starting to type in the search bar at Instagram and note the auto-complete drop-down list of popular tags. Instagram's auto-complete comes from actual searches.
- Save all your hashtags in a text file or spreadsheet. Separate them by niches, products, people, or other categories. When you need hashtags, just go to your file and copy them.
- Use hashtags used by communities related to your product's niche.

Find popular hashtags related to your niche using the following apps:
- keywordtool.io
- displaypurposes.com
- skedsocial.com
- hashtagify.me
- all-hashtag.com
- AutoHash is a mobile app that analyzes your images and suggests hashtags.

Where to Place Hashtags

- As a sticker on your images and videos
- Your post's description
- Comments you leave
- Comments you get
- Your Instagram stories
- Your profile bio

Tips for Posting

- When someone likes or comments on your image posts, send them a thank you. It's a natural way to start a conversation.
- If your creative muse takes a vacation, post other people's content.
- Study the posts of the most popular Instagram profiles in your niche. Look for content that attracted the most comments. This is a great way to get inspired for what you could post.
- Follow the followers of other sellers in your niche. If they appear to be frequent or recent posters, start liking their images. Many of them will follow you back.
- Follow Etsy sellers with complementary product lines to yours. Comment and like their content. Message them and see if they would like to cross-promote each other's lines.
- Post often. Uploading content twice a day has shown to increase followers. Use one of the social media scheduling tools described earlier.
- Instagram is highly social. Tagging others (adding @ personsusername) can earn goodwill and increase your post comments.
- Get even more followers from your popular posts with Instagram advertising, explained in Chapter 18.

Chapter 15

Twitter Tips

T witter has over 300 million users who produce 500 million tweets every day. Eighty percent of Twitter users live outside the US, yet twenty-four percent of Americans use the site. Etsy's Twitter feed has over 2 million followers.

Setting Up Business Account

- As with your other social accounts, choose a username / handle or close version of your business name that helps identify your brand.
- Set up a Twitter business account (or convert your personal account) to take advantage of extra features.

Selling on Twitter

Selling on Twitter is as simple as tweeting with a link to an item in your Etsy or other online shopping cart. However, before you start pitching everyone, create lists of potential buyers using Twitter Lists. For instance, your most important list will be previous customers.

Growing Your Following

- Search Twitter for popular influencers in your niche and other sellers with products like yours. If you sell accessories, type in what kind, like "handbags", in the search bar at Twitter.com. On the sidebar, Twitter suggests "Who to Follow." As you follow some, Twitter continues to show more in your interests.

- Bloggers use Twitter to announce their newest posts. Use Twitter to find bloggers who review products like yours.
- Follow leaders in your field (those with lots of followers) and follow their followers. As long as your Tweets are helpful or entertaining, many will follow you back.
- Seek popular Twitter users in related niches. For example, if you sell repurposed clothing or accessories, identify big influencers in fashion to follow. Going sustainable is trending in the fashion world.
- When entering or starting conversations on Twitter, aim for engagement. You'll grow your influence faster with genuine connections rather than just blasting out promotional tweets.

Tweets

- Tweet directly from Etsy when you publish a new product listing, get a five-star review, or offer a coupon. See Shop Manager > Marketing > Social media.
- Learn the best time of the day to tweet with a tool like Tweriod.com.
- Posting on Twitter teaches you how to focus your message. Tweets are limited to 280 characters.
- Tweeting is another way to engage through dialog. It's like sending brief instant messages.
- Frequent tweets generate more followers. Use social posting tools like Hootsuite or Buffer to schedule when your messages go out.
- Mix your tweet content; seven helpful or entertaining tweets for every one tweet about your products. If that feels too pushy, try ten to one (promo).
- Tweets with images get more engagement. This rule is true on most social media sites.
- Statistically, Tweets with links get more clicks.

- Use Twitter Analytics to learn which of your tweets get the most engagement.
- Tweetdeck.twitter.com lets you manage all your Twitter activity.

Hashtags

- Hashtags (putting the # sign before a keyword tag) in Twitter work like they do in Instagram.
- Using two relevant hashtags in a tweet gets more engagement.
- See the section on Instagram hashtags as the same guidelines apply on Twitter.

Automatically post tweets from your Etsy store using the Etsy-approved app Etsy-fu: https://etsyapps.com/etsy-fu/

As you have learned from the last several chapters, there are many options for selling online beyond Etsy or Amazon. If your sales have been on the rise and you feel ready to scale up your business, the next chapter tells you about Shopify and other multichannel listing tools.

Chapter 16

Selling with Shopify and Multichannel Listing Apps

Feeling a little overwhelmed with all the ways you could sell online? As mentioned earlier, the solution is to choose one platform, get good at it, and then take on another, and then another.

But what's the next step when you have mastered selling on Etsy and Amazon and you are ready to expand across multiple markets? This chapter introduces Shopify and other seller tools that help you get your product listings on different platforms from one interface. They are often referred to as "multichannel listing software."

Shopify and other apps for syncing products across multiple sites are subscription-based services. Some offer free trials so you can test the waters before subscribing.

How do you know if you are ready for multichannel listing software? A rough guideline is when your sales pass $800 to $1,000 a month and show a steady, upward trend. This is the level where your gig starts looking like an actual business and increased sales justify the added cost of using advanced tools for increasing distribution.

Multichannel distribution lets you access giant e-commerce platforms like Amazon, Walmart, and Google as well as Etsy. There are important differences among selling platforms to keep in mind:

- **Shopper demographics.** Just because you can access a giant sales platform doesn't mean you should. Walmart attracts bargain hunters who won't appreciate the value of handmade items.

- **Competitors**. The Amazon marketplace is full of sellers of cheaply made imports from other countries. Whereas, the Amazon Handmade market is a subset selling area where there may be less competition, depending on what you make.
- **Seller fees**. Commissions you pay per sale differ from site to site. Etsy charges 5%, while Amazon charges 15% per sale. Pay attention to your ROI (Return on Investment) for each site to ensure you remain profitable. Know your cost of goods and cost of sales before signing up to sell on a platform.
- **Returns**. Almost all selling platforms want sellers to offer a return policy. Your sales will improve if you offer a money-back guarantee, say for two weeks or longer, starting upon the delivery date.

Useful features to look for from multi-platform selling apps include:
- Synchronize inventory across multiple sites so you don't oversell what you have in stock.
- Easily import / export listings from one platform to another.
- Edit or update listings on all channels at the same time.
- Manage shipping from all channels from one interface.
- Reporting insights that let you know how platforms are performing.
- Support with issues and glitches.
- Sync with Amazon FBA inventory to fulfill and ship orders from other channels.

Shopify

Shopify is a popular suite of tools that let you sell your products online through many marketplaces. It allows you to customize a shopping cart from pre-designed themes with no need for skills or previous experience in building a website.

Shopify integrates with Amazon, Etsy, eBay, Google, Instagram, Facebook, Pinterest, Lyst, your own website and many other platforms.

Shopify is a monthly subscription service, starting at a basic level for $29 a month. At what point in your business will Shopify be profitable?

Let's say you sell on Etsy, where there is no monthly fee. You pay 5% per sale and $.20 per listing. Your sales on Etsy are $600 a month, for which you are paying at least $30 a month in commissions (not counting listing fees.) Five percent of $600 is $30, which is equal to a month's subscription for Shopify. In this example, you would want a minimum monthly volume exceeding $600 before considering Shopify.

Etsy vs Shopify

A frequently asked question about e-commerce for handmade products is "should I sell my items through Etsy or Shopify?" It's like comparing apples to oranges. The question should be "at what point in my business growth should I consider Shopify over Etsy?"

Etsy is a marketplace with a search engine and shopping cart, serving a large, loyal audience of shoppers. Etsy's fan base grows from the work of its marketing team whose mission is to get shoppers coming to the site and help sellers make sales.

Shopify is an integrative shopping cart app allowing you to sell on multiple platforms, but there is no marketplace of Shopify buyers.

On Etsy your products are displayed to shoppers looking to buy handmade, whereas with Shopify, you have to find customers and send them to your checkout page. You do that through SEO (getting visitors organically from search) or through paid ads.

Pros of Using Shopify

- Flexible. It integrates with over 2,000 platforms including Etsy, Facebook, Pinterest, Instagram, Google Shopping, eBay, Amazon, Woo Commerce, and print-on-demand services like Printful. https://apps.shopify.com/
- Shopify lets you sell digital downloads directly using one of their free apps: https://apps.shopify.com/digital-downloads
- You don't need previous experience in website building. With Shopify, you can "drag and drop" or choose from many templates.
- Customize your website checkout pages, unlike on Etsy or Amazon.
- Scalable. Think of Etsy when you are starting your hand-made business. When it's time to scale up, Shopify is the app to expand your e-commerce presence on all the major social media platforms through a single interface.
- Customer support for reaching someone to help you answer questions and resolve issues.

Cons of Using Shopify

- If you don't have a customer base already, you'll have to work harder to get eyes on your product listings.
- If you are a startup, you will need to budget an additional expense per month (basic plan around $29, advanced features for $79 and $299) than you would starting with an Etsy store (no monthly fee, no set up fee, and only $.20 per listing.)
- Lots of functions require installing extra apps.
- You need one of the higher-priced subscriptions to get advanced features like professional reports.
- Though some SEO tactics work with Shopify, optimizing product pages is not as easy as with Etsy or Amazon.
- Product images have to fit the same aspect ratio.

Example of how to expand your Etsy or Amazon Handmade business by adding Shopify integrations. As mentioned above, Shopify will be more useful when you are ready to expand or scale up your existing sales from Etsy or Amazon. You need enough profit coming in to justify paying the extra cost of a Shopify subscription and then be ready to grow traffic to make that subscription pay off from increased sales volume.

Growing your traffic can happen in several ways. For example, Pinterest attracts millions of visitors who use the site to research ideas before making a purchase. With the Shopify Pinterest integration, you can add a buy button to a pin promoting one of your products. Visitors see your image / pin. If it matches (is relevant to) their needs, they can click the buy button and check out from your Shopify page. As you build your Pinterest following, it's an easy step to add the Shopify buy button to your pins.

Both Facebook Shops and Instagram Shops integrate with Shopify similarly to Pinterest. If you promote your products on these sites, visitors can click on the buy button to order and pay for a purchase. Like with Pinterest, if you have an Instagram or FB following, growing your business through these social accounts is much easier using Shopify.

Let's not forget Google. Say you have done a good job with your SEO and your product pages are showing up in Google Shopping search results. By integrating with Shopify, potential customers are one click away from buying after seeing your product on Google Shopping.

More Apps for Selling on Multiple Platforms

Besides Shopify, here are other multichannel listing services:
- An Etsy-approved app for selling directly from Facebook and Instagram through your Etsy shop is Spreesy: https://etsyapps.com/spreesy/
- https://sellbery.com integrates with Amazon, Etsy, eBay, Google Shopping, Facebook, and more.
- https://www.sellbrite.com/ integrates with Amazon, Etsy,

eBay, Google, Sears, and more.
*   https://www.primaseller.com/ integrates with Amazon, Etsy, eBay, and Flipkart.

Syncing Listing Data Between Platforms

While selling the same product line on multiple platforms sounds appealing, there are a couple of tech steps to master. They aren't difficult and all tools make ease of operation a priority. YouTube video tutorials walk you through what's needed.

A summary of the process: using a product data feed, a seller can quickly import or export product listings to other sites. The product data field comprises various elements in your listing Viewers to your pages don't see the data feed, as it's in the background. But apps know how to look for these feeds, extract the appropriate field data and export it to another platform.

When you are connecting two or more shops through one app, you may be asked to identify data fields and relate them to the platforms you want to sell in. For instance, in your Etsy data file, your product listing description data may have a different name than the Amazon product listing description field. If a tool cannot match these automatically, it will prompt you to map the two fields so they sync before importing.

With your product listings live on multiple channels, it's time to attract more visitors. A powerful way to get more traffic is getting influencers and the media to mention or review your products. The next chapter tells you how to find and pitch influencers, bloggers, and reporters.

Chapter 17

Get Influencers to Mention Your Products

With a catchy pitch to the right influencer, your hand-made products could get mentions resulting in sales from popular blogs, Instagram feeds, Pinterest boards, podcasts, magazines, or other media.

In this chapter, you will learn how to get publicity based on your story. You will discover:

* How to prepare before reaching out to influencers
* Types of influencer media
* How to pitch your story
* Where to find influencer and media contacts
* Tips for getting publicity

How to Prepare Before Reaching out to Influencers

One study showed that ninety percent of journalists begin story research by searching online. If they find you and your story is newsworthy, they will write about you.

Before you reach out to a reporter, blogger, or product reviewer, learn if they are a fit for your product line. Have they reviewed or mentioned handmade products like yours previously? If your item isn't relevant to their audience, they either won't be interested, or if they take your money to mention our product, you won't get sales.

Before you reach out to influencers, have an online media kit you can refer them to. Here is a list of what your media kit should include. If you don't have all of these, create a media kit from what you have. Even a few of these are better than nothing.

- The first thing to **get clear about is your message**. What's your story, your background, your vision/mission? You need a seven-word version, a one-paragraph version, and a longer bio of your journey as a maker or artisan.
- A downloadable, bulleted **fact sheet of who you are**, what you do, where you live, when you got started, how you make your crafts, and your contact information.
- **"About me" page**. The story of your background, education, awards, and anything pertinent to your craft. Avoid listing your complete job history unless a position specifically applied to developing your handmade products.
- **High resolution, professional-looking photos** of you, you making your crafts, and several of your best-looking pieces.
- **Video** of you making or talking about your indie designs.
- **News release** about you and your work.
- **Previous media mentions**: interviews, articles, press clips, or reviews.
- **Awards or competitions** you have won.
- List of ten or twelve **sample questions for an interview**.
- If you have them, include jokes or **fun facts**.
- Your **contact information**.

Types of Influencers and Media

Publicity takes many forms including mention in newspapers, magazines, TV, and online media such as blogs, podcasts, videos, and social site posts. As mentioned earlier, identify influencers who have written about similar items to those you make.

When you get written about in one or more media, mention that when pitching other influencers.

Social Influencers

Influencers on Instagram, Facebook, Twitter, Pinterest or YouTube produce content exposed to thousands—even hundreds of thousands—of followers. Social monitoring tools like Influence.co/category/etsy, Heepsy.com and NinjaOutreach.com locate them for you. Though all are subscription services, you can sign up for a month, find lists of influencers in your genre to pitch, and then cancel.

Invest time studying each influencer's past posts and discovering the kinds of products they mention. Do their past posts include products like yours?

Influencers can be divided between macro and micro-influencers. The average small business owner can't afford to pay the fees macro-influencers charge. But hiring micro-influencers, whose audiences number between 1,000 and 100,000, won't break the bank.

Bloggers Who Review Handmade Products

Shopping bloggers review new indie-made products—some for a fee, some for a free product. Before you pitch a blogger, read their past posts and get familiar with how they've written about other products like yours.

Besides reviews, bloggers mention product giveaways or contests. If a blogger agrees to write about your items, they will include a link to your store. A contest can drive new visitors to your Etsy or online store.

The more popular the blog, the more requests they get to review products. Your pitch can stand out by:
- Addressing the blogger by name
- Praising one or two of their past posts that you like
- Providing brilliant images of your work
- Offering to link to them from your blog or social feed
- Being authentic. Tell your story. People love stories they can relate to.

The following blogs have reviewed handmade products. If one of these looks like a match for what you make, study their past reviews, send them a brief pitch, and request their product submission guidelines.

- WhoWhatWear.com/indie-fashion-brands
- Ohjoy.blogs.com
- Coolmompicks.com
- Mightygoods.com
- Weheartthis.com
- Indiefixx.com
- Tryhandmade.com
- Wickedlychic.com
- Hearthandmadeblog.com
- Mixedplateblog.com

Shopping review blogs for consumer brands:

- Shopstyle.com
- Thisnext.com
- Iliketotallyloveit.com
- Shefinds.com

Newspapers and Magazines

If you make a good pitch and your photos are interesting, local newspapers, magazines, and TV affiliate stations are likely to mention you because you are part of the community.

Most national media like newspapers and magazines look for stories that inform, educate, provoke, or entertain their readers. When you can supply editors with news or stories that relate to the interests of their audiences, you have made their jobs easier. The key is pitching reporters that have covered stories like yours. Finding contact information for the media is described later in this chapter.

How to Pitch Your Story

The job of editors, writers, reporters and producers is finding stories to develop for their audiences. They get lots of pitches from product sellers every day and reject most.

Media reporters can look at a pitch or news release and determine in seconds if it's right for their readers or viewers. The key phrase is "their readers or viewers." This is where most pitches fail. The message or product is too self-promotional or isn't a fit for their audience. If you want someone in the media to mention you, learn all you can about what stories they write about.

Start your pitch by letting the person know how you found them and why you enjoy their content. Follow with a paragraph or two and a link to a longer news release on your website's online media kit.

Your pitch should be a brief enough introduction to your story that the editor is intrigued but not overwhelmed with too much information. State a problem that your handmade item solves. For example, if you make home décor items from repurposed plastic, you are helping save the planet by re-using plastic that would otherwise add to landfills. Describe your solution. Then link readers to your website, Facebook page, or blog for more information.

Part of your story is visual, so you will want to include your best images and/or video if you have it. If the person you are pitching wants to know more, they will contact you.

You may be asked to provide the reviewer a free product sample.

Where to Find Influencers and Media Contacts

Influencers and media contacts could be writers, reporters, bloggers, producers, podcasters, and editors. Below are many ways to find them.

Start with a **Google search**. For example, if you make a

line of accessories for the Western wear audience, search for "western fashion bloggers."

As mentioned earlier, **Heepsy** is one of the many (and most affordable) social listening tools offering both free and paid subscription options. Use them to find social media influencers by their audience, reach, and engagement.

Collabfluence.com is a monthly subscription service where you can post an ad about your product and let influencers come to you. You describe your handmade product line, the amount you are willing to pay for a post or mention, and your contact information.

Google.com/alerts programs Google to send you alerts when any news appears about products like those you make. I programmed multiple Google alerts to notify about "sustainable fashion" and several other topics. Make a note of the reporter or blogger's name and find their contact information.

Locate blogs **by category** at:

- Feedly.com
- Blogarama.com
- Bloggernity.com
- Alltop.com

Twitter and **Instagram** help you locate editors, producers, bloggers, and reviewers. In the search bar, type in the name or hashtag of the media and hit enter. On Twitter, choose the "People" tab. For example, typing HGTV brings up show producers and reporters and what topics they cover. Also search by job title. For instance, search for "product reviewer" and start following reviewers who cover products like yours. A survey reported that forty-six percent of journalists receive story pitches through Twitter.

USNPL.com is a free-to-access directory of newspaper reporters in the US.

For **print publications**, magazine mastheads list the publisher, editor and other staff including editors who cover specific sections like New Products, Startups, etc.

HelpAReporter.com (HARO) is a free newsletter sending out lists of media reporters looking for stories on an enormous variety of topics. You can subscribe to receive one or more lists around broad topics. One topic that may be useful to makers is the "Giftbag" list.

More Tips for Getting Publicity

- Follow and read the publications, news feeds, blogs, or watch the TV shows to which you are thinking of pitching your story.
- Target media outlets and reporters relevant to your work. If you make hair bows for young girls, don't contact a writer for Popular Mechanics.
- Discover if they have already reviewed businesses like yours.
- Search for the "New Products" section of a publication. These departments are always looking for cool new stuff for their readers.
- Pictures and videos tell stories. Reporters look for interesting visuals accompanying news releases.
- Whenever you come out with a new product, send out a news release. Send a product sample to local newspapers and TV networks.
- Announce any awards you have just won. Local newspapers like to feature independent businesses that receive recognition as it looks great for the community.
- Write a story if where you work is in a historic or unusual location.
- Take advantage of holiday gift buying. Feature editors look for stories ahead of holidays.
- Can you relate your items to special days or months? November 15 is America Recycles Day. Find more interesting facts about each month of the year at gone-ta-pott.com/facts-about-each-month-directory.html.

- Donate a piece you make to a charitable cause or charity fundraiser. Send a news release to local newspapers, magazines, and TV shows with a photo of your piece.
- Sponsor a local community event and publicize it to local newspapers.
- Reporters are always looking for news items that tie into what's being read and talked about in the mainstream media. Can you link a popular topic to your product line?
- At the end of your pitch to the media, link to your online media kit.

Start collecting any mentions of you by influencers or the media. It will make you proud of what you are creating. This collection should appear in your website's media kit. If you plan to grow your brand and sell to boutiques, you'll find a portfolio of press clippings can be very persuasive when approaching stores.

You have learned many ways to market your handmade items online. After you have sales coming in, and only after, consider scaling up your business through ads. The next chapter tells you how.

Chapter 18

Running Paid Ads

Most social platforms and e-commerce sites have advertising programs. This chapter helps you determine if paid advertising is right for you.

With so many free ways to promote online, use them first before putting money into paid ads. Only after you have extra income coming in, should you consider risking money testing ad campaigns.

Though ad programs will vary from site to site, below are important best practices to remember before running ads on any site:

- Test ads only after you know your product listing page does its job of converting visitors to buyers. If your pages are getting traffic but not converting, look at improving your images, your SEO keyword relevancy, your product description, and your price. When you start getting sales from organic traffic, you can scale up your page's profits with ads.
- Set a low daily budget and gradually raise ad spending only as long as you see a profit. Some sites let you spend as little as $1 a day.
- Calculate your profit margins before testing ads.
- Target your audience(s) to match the theme or media you craft with. For instance, if you sell handmade clothing or accessories, your audiences will be found on style and fashion review sites or Pinterest boards.
- Test ads using different search terms to learn which phrases convert more searchers to buyers.

- Regardless of where you advertise, monitor your ad campaigns so you can know which ads are generating sales.

Etsy Ads

Etsy sellers have the option of paying for "Etsy Ads," a feature under "Marketing" in your "Shop Manager." But as mentioned, only test "Etsy Ads" after you have had organic sales.

Choose listings you want to promote and set a daily spending budget. Set your initial budget at the minimum so you can affordably test results. Etsy lets you budget as low as $1 per day. After a few weeks, go back in and view your promoted listings statistics.

Etsy doesn't offer any find tuning of ad campaigns. You turn the "Promoted Listings" feature on, select which of your listings to promote, and set a daily budget. You only pay when someone clicks through from an ad to your product listing.

Amazon Handmade Ads

To test ads on Amazon for your listings in Amazon Handmade, login to your account at https://sellercentral.amazon.com/ Click on the "Advertising" tab and from the drop down, select "Campaign Manager."

After you start an ad campaign, you can view your ad's impressions, clicks, click-through rates, ad spend, CPC (Cost Per Click), orders, sales, and ACOS (Advertising Cost of Sales.)

Amazon ads require a minimum daily budget of $5. Know your profit margins before testing ads on Amazon.

Amazon has several options for targeting shoppers, divided into automatic and manual targeting:

Automatic targeting – Amazon chooses how and when to display your ad based on its title and description

Manual targeting – You choose among:
- Target specific keywords. These should match the keywords in your product listing title and description.

Researching keywords is explained in Chapter 6.
- Target specific products. You can program your ad to show when someone is viewing your competitor's listings.
- Target specific categories. You can target whole categories, like jewelry, accessories, men's clothes, etc.

Amazon lets you select broad, phrase, exact, and negative match types when setting up your ads. Save money and get more useful data by choosing phrase and exact matching. Choosing broad tells Amazon to show your ads when viewers type in words similar to yours, therefore spending more of your money on related phrases.

When beginning ads on Amazon, set up an automatic targeting campaign to run with a minimum budget. Let it run for a few days to a week. Then, go into your campaign manager and view the results to learn which search terms people used to click through on your ads. Then, create a new keyword ad campaign targeting those search terms in a manual targeting campaigns.

Depending on your budget, you can run several types of ads at the same time for a week. For instance, you could set up one ad on automatic targeting, another for keywords, another for category, and another targeting your competitors. After the ads run for seven days, examine the results to decide whether to continue running ads (if they resulted in sales) or pause them (because they didn't get sales.)

Facebook and Instagram Ads

Facebook owns Instagram and managing ads for both platforms starts on FB. FB offers precise targeting options for showing ads on the two sites. Start by setting up a Facebook Business Manager account at https://business.facebook.com/.
- Determine your daily budget. FB lets you limit your daily ad spend to $1 or more.
- Determine what you want people to do after viewing your ad. Join your mailing list? Buy your product?

- If you have your own website, add a Facebook Pixel code to the website landing page you send people to. The pixel collects data you can use for advanced targeting in ads.
- Use your best images, or better yet, use videos in your ads, as video ads get a better response rate.
- Limit the amount of text. Most viewers are skimming their feeds and won't read lengthy paragraphs.
- Include a call to action. Tell viewers what to do, like "click here to order."
- Target an audience that likes the FB pages of sellers of products like yours.
- Target people who like FB pages that are likely to buy products like yours. If you sell handmade jewelry, you can have your ads show to people who liked fashion pages on FB.
- Target specific keywords and FB will show you which FB pages match.
- Upload emails of your customers and tell FB to create a look-alike audience based on common demographics.
- Monitor your ad analytics through your FB Business Manager dashboard: https://business.facebook.com
- For an overview of setting up ads on FB, see: https://www.facebook.com/business/ads
- Like with Facebook ads, you can create look-alike audiences for Instagram ads through your Facebook Business Manager site.
- Monitor your Etsy shop stats closely when you run an Instagram or other ad campaign. Your Etsy stats will tell you if you are getting traffic from Instagram or other social networks. If ads are working, increase your budget and try new audiences.
- If your ads do not result in profitable sales, stop the campaigns. Change your content, or your offer, or your audience.

Pinterest Ads

Pinterest offers several options for ads. First, create or switch to a business account at: http://pinterest.com/business/create/

- From your business account dashboard, Click "Ads" and then "Create Ads."
- Click "New ad group"
- Click "Targeting"
- Under "Keywords" (below "Add interests") type in your keywords. Pinterest will auto-suggest keywords based on searches.
- Choose other demographics like age and gender.
- Enter your daily budget.
- Enter the duration of your ad campaign.
- Choose the pin you want to promote. You can promote images or videos.
- Choose the destination URL you want visitors to go to.
- For more details, see Pinterest's Ad Manager at https://business.pinterest.com/en/using-ads-manager

Influencer Paid Posts

Influencer marketing has become a major force in advertising. Huge companies pay lots of money to popular influencers to promote their brands. Costs range from $25 to thousands per post, depending on the size of the influencer's audience.

For the handmaker, many of the agencies that manage paid influencer campaigns will be out of reach financially. The solution is to look for micro-influencers with smaller audiences, but lower costs per post.

Searching Instagram for hashtags related to your niche will get you the top posts that include your hashtag. For instance, if you make wedding favors, search for #handmadeweddings or #handmadeweddingfavors. Click on the images to view the poster's profile and website to learn if they post for pay.

Refer to Chapter 17 for more about how to find and pitch influencers whose viewers match your product's genre.

Track Your Ad Results

The platforms above provide data on how your ads are performing, though it may take a few days to a week to get enough results to make any decisions. After measuring your results, you can run more ads proved to yield sales, tweak ads to test again, and eventually weed out the losers.

Ads aren't for every handmade product. Remember:

- Only run ads to scale up your sales after your listings prove they can convert organic traffic into sales.
- Set a low minimum daily budget when testing ads.
- Track and measure ad performance closely to learn if it's worth increasing ad spend or turning it off.

Let's face it, no matter how much you know, unexpected stuff can throw your well-laid plans into chaos. The last chapter will help you avoid pitfalls many sellers make.

Chapter 19

Pitfalls to Avoid

This chapter is a collection of common mistakes that can limit your handmade business growth online. Some of these points may have appeared elsewhere in the book, but they are worth repeating.

* Setting up an online shop and then sitting back to wait for people to start buying. Presuming you used good images, popular search terms from SEO research, and compelling product descriptions, it still may take several weeks before your listings show up in search results. If you are selling from your own website, you have to drive buyers to your listings.

* Using poor quality images. You've already heard this many times. See Chapter 3 for how to correct your images.

* Failing to have a returns policy is the same as telling the customer that you do not accept returns if she is unhappy. Not accepting returns can cost you a lot of business because shoppers don't want to take the risk. Would you?

* Pricing your handmade items too low. People will pay more for handmade items. It is important to remember you are not in competition with WalMart.

* Not reading and following an online site's policies for sellers can be costly. If you violate their terms, it does not matter that you did not know the rules, they may still shut you down.

* Double check your content for spelling or grammatical errors in your descriptive text. Shoppers may think that if you are not paying attention to your writing, you may make mistakes in your crafting, too.

* Using text in your content that no one is searching for. Use the resources mentioned in Chapter 6 to research words and phrases consumers use to find products like yours.

* Exaggerated shipping or handling costs is an obvious attempt to exploit your customer. Online shoppers are savvy. It's okay to recover your actual shipping costs, but avoid overcharging. It's even better to offer free shipping if you can afford it.

* Thinking you have learned everything there is to know can cost you in the long run. Online markets and technology changes so much that the only constant is change. There's always more to explore and experiment with. The most successful sellers maintain that they never stop learning.

* Failing to pay attention to what your customers say when leaving reviews and commenting on social posts. My most successful product line earned over $134,00 in sales, mainly because I listened to buyers' feedback. Customers told me which colors they liked, how they planned to give the item as a gift, and how they would wear the piece. I tweaked my product line, packaging, and display based on comments from shoppers and sales went up.

* Getting attached to wins. Success can create an illusion that one can't fail. But technology changes, as does product demand. The solution is to always be thinking of your next product line or a new market to expand into.

* Not keeping up with changes in e-commerce sites. Subscribe to my free newsletter to get news and updates about selling crafts online. Subscribe at https://craftmarketer.com/newsletter/

The Appendices that follow give you more resources to help grow your handmade business.

APPENDICES

Appendix 1

How to Create Product Descriptions That Sell

When marketing your handmade items online, words and images have to do the selling. Product descriptions play a key role in converting shoppers to buyers. Check out how the top sellers on Etsy and Amazon Handmade describe their handmade products by:

For viewing the top selling Etsy shops, visit EtsyRank.com. Choose the category closest to your product line. Identify some of the best sellers in your category. Click through and check out their shops and product descriptions.

For viewing the top selling Amazon Handmade shops, visit https://www.amazon.com/Best-Sellers-Handmade/zgbs/handmade. Amazon shows you the top sellers and you can drill down into categories to find products like yours. Click through to view the top selling products' listings for examples of their listing descriptions.

Here are elements common to product listing descriptions that sell:

- Short bullet points instead of long paragraphs of text. Shoppers don't read long blocks of text (especially on mobile phones which probably account for half of your viewers) but they will scan bullet points.
- Authentic language. Write from your own voice rather than copy others' words.
- State who the product is for. Is it for men, women, young girls, or who exactly needs it.
- Your points should answer all the important questions

about your product like: colors, weight, dimensions, packaging, assembly, how-to-care-for, and how-to-travel-with.

- Include a bullet point describing materials used.
- If your materials or packaging is environmentally friendly, include a bullet point describing how.
- Include benefits like is your product versatile, in style, fun, simple to use, or make your life easier in some way?
- Use words that describe how customers will feel: warm, cozy, delicious, aromatic, satisfying, fulfilled, enchanted, flattered.
- I offer free shipping and Etsy posts a badge on my listings letting customers know. But I also include "Free shipping to US addresses" among my description bullet list.
- Etsy provides a link to your reviews near the top of your listing, but you can also add your best review quote(s) to your description area.
- Add a call-to-action before your links, like "Shop now at....."
- Invite shoppers to contact you anytime with questions about the product.
- Spellcheck and proofread your description. If your copy contains typos and misspellings, what do you think the shopper is going to imagine about your product?

Finally, include a call to action. Up-sell and cross-sell in your descriptions. Add links to related products in your shop and another link to your shop main page. When you are shopping on Amazon or Etsy you'll see messages like "Customers who bought this, also bought this...." or "Frequently bought with....."

Appendix 2

Online Channels for Selling Wholesale to Stores

Selling to stores is not for everyone, but for those who have the production capacity and the profit margin (stores typically want a 50 percent discount,) selling wholesale can grow into a big business.

Before you venture into this area, you should know exactly how much it costs you (labor and materials) to produce your craft pieces to know if you can make a profit selling wholesale. See Chapter 4.

Wholesale buyers want to work with professionals. Review Chapter 2 for how to set up your brand to make the best impression when approaching stores.

Wholesale buying portals. The websites below act as online portals where independent retail store buyers can purchase directly from makers. Each site has its own terms for listing products:

- Stockabl.com
- Tundra.com
- Faire.com
- Indieme.com
- LAShowroom.com
- Wholesaleinabox.com
- Trouva.com (UK)
- QVC.com — QVC is the most popular home shopping network. Working with QVC requires large inventories so consider them only if you have reliable production capacity in place. See their site for vendor information.

Alternatives to Etsy and Amazon Handmade

Though Etsy and Amazon Handmade have the largest global audience of buyers for handmade products, there are many other sites around the world to sell from.

US & Canada
- artfire.com
- zibbet.com
- bonanza.com
- artfulhome.com
- ecrater.com
- houzz.com
- makersmarket.us
- uncommongoods.com
- icraftgifts.com
- latitudesdecor.com

UK
- thefuturekept.com
- folksy.com
- madebyhandonline.com
- misi.co.uk
- miratis.com
- designersmakers.com
- designnation.co.uk
- aerende.co.uk
- personalise.co.uk

- thecraftersbarn.co.uk
- notonthehighstreet.com
- rebelsmarket.com
- artsthread.com
- affordablebritishart.co.uk
- art2arts.co.uk
- artclickireland.com

Europe
- artbaazar.com
- artebooking.com
- zet.gallery

Australia
- madeit.com.au
- stateoftheartgallery.com.au
- artloversaustralia.com.au
- artpharmacy.com.au

India and Asia
- melaartisans.com
- artisera.com
- artzyme.com
- lazada.com (Southeast Asia)

International
- artsyshark.com/sell-art-online-directory/
- eclecticartisans.com (handmade jewelry)

Facebook Marketplace is currently available to people over 18 in the US, the UK, Australia, New Zealand and Mexico on the Facebook app.

Where to Sell On-Demand-Products with Your Designs

Suppose you have creative ideas but you don't want to make items to sell. You can get your artwork and designs printed on popular products like calendars, posters, mousepads, t-shirts, aprons, cutting boards and many others by what's called on-demand manufacturing.

In this chapter, you will find the most popular places online that automate the whole design-to-product-to-payment-to-customer cycle. If this way of marketing art and design appeals to you, the sites here have systems in place to create and sell products on demand.

Printful.com — Printful is an on-demand order fulfillment and warehousing service that fulfills and ships products including clothing, accessories, and home & living items for online businesses.

Cafepress.com — Upload your art and sell it on t-shirts, apparel, gifts for the home, stationery, gear, and other stuff that gets printed on. You set the retail price. They pay you the difference between your price and a base cost.

Zazzle.com — Make money by selling your ideas on products. Shoppers browse the catalog and when an order is placed, the product is made and shipped. Add your designs to more than twenty-five different kinds of products.

Redbubble.com — This is an online art gallery that makes it easy to sell your art, photos, designs and illustrations as framed prints, mounted prints, greeting cards, posters, designer t-shirts and more. Sign up for free, then upload your artwork. They collect the orders, deduct a base price for making products, and send your earnings to you.

Spreadshirt.com — Got designs for shirts? This site specializes in turning your art into shirt wear; it's free to set up, free to sell from. Artists earn a commission upon sales. Premium membership available at a monthly fee.

Ponoko.com — You can sell your products and products by setting up your own showroom here for free. You can also edit and mashup product plans you download from Ponoko to sell something original, as long as you abide by the designer's copyright license. You set the prices.

Printfection.com — Here, it's free to set up a store where customers can order your designs made onto products like t-shirts, mousepads, cutting boards, aprons and more. Each product has a base price and you add your desired markup to come to the selling price.

Artsnow.com — Artsnow lets you build an online store and display products made from your art or design. Choose from more than 200 products, ranging from clothing and accessories to home and office commodities. No up front charges or inventory investment. They make and ship products upon demand.

Artwanted.com — This is an artist community where artists and photographers can interact with each other and sell their artwork. The site has over 145,000 images that can be printed to a variety of print sizes and products like calendars, print books, posters, t-shirts, etc.

Greetingcarduniverse.com — Get your art on to greeting cards here and sell them through your own free store. You retain copyright to your images. Artists earn up to $0.56 for each paper card sold. .

Imagekind.com — Imagekind is an art site offering fine art images for sale as framed and poster art created from your art. They offer several options for creating a storefront.

Deviantart.com — Deviantart is an online art community for artists and art lovers to interact in a variety of ways. A community account is free. Additional promotional features require a subscription fee. Art and design can be transferred to media such as mugs, jigsaw puzzles, canvases, calendars, mouse pads, coasters, postcards, and magnets. Users earn 50 percent of the profits above a pre-set base cost.

About the Author

James Dillehay is a craft artisan, former gallery owner, and author of fifteen books. He has sold his handmade products online at Etsy, Ebay, and Amazon, at competitive juried shows in the US, and to galleries and boutiques from Manhattan to the Grand Canyon.

James developed and presented crafts marketing programs for the University of Alaska, Northern New Mexico Community College, Bootcamp for Artists and Craftspeople, The Learning Annex, and more.

He has been interviewed in The Wall Street Journal Online, Yahoo Finance, Bottom Line Personal, Family Circle, The Crafts Report, Working Mothers, Entrepreneur Radio, HGTV's The Carol Duvall Show, and more.

James currently lives, writes, and creates cool stuff from a studio he built himself (and it doesn't leak) next to a national forest in New Mexico.

Tap into James' craft business experience through his free newsletter at Craftmarketer.com and get the free bonus ebook described on pages 2 and 121.

What's Your Next Step?

Are your handmade goods struggling to find buyers? Learn effective tactics to make that cash register ring.

How to Price Crafts and Things You Make to Sell is a modern-day roadmap for rate-setting strategies in the competitive handmade-products industry. With oodles of real-world examples, James Dillehay's time-tested techniques will help you refine your presentation and understand your market to hit the monetary sweet spot.

And by following his commonsense approach, the fruits of your labor will reach an excited audience eagerly clamoring for your next masterpiece.

In ***How to Price Crafts and Things You Make to Sell,*** you'll discover:

+ Pricing strategies for crafts that make money
+ Innovative ways to make your handcrafted wares stand out over other sellers
+ How to set prices higher while keeping shoppers clicking that buy button
+ Logical approaches to position "one-of-a-kind" items in the premium dollar range
+ Methods for spotting trends to skyrocket profits, and much, much more!

How to Price Crafts and Things You Make to Sell is a no-nonsense guidebook for anyone looking to optimize their online venture. If you like straightforward direction, experience-based suggestions, and filling your coffers to overflowing, then you'll love James Dillehay's treasure trove of advice.

Get your copy today.

Free Ebook Reveals Blueprint Used by
Top Sellers to Boost Sales + Profits

Looking for a *blueprint for selling your handmade products*? I wish I had one back in those early years of struggling with unknowns, false starts, and misdirections.

What if you could bypass those startup pains and grow your sales and profits, faster and easier? Now, you can with the ***Blueprint for Selling Handmade Products*** ebook.

It outlines **proven tips** from over twenty years of selling handmade items in multiple markets.

Download this gift from the author. Get your **free** ebook (PDF) now at: **Craftmarketer.com/bp/**

Made in the USA
Las Vegas, NV
02 September 2022

54585865R00069